What's Next?

WHAT'S NEXT?

ERNEST GORDON
and PETER FUNK

LOGOS INTERNATIONAL
PLAINFIELD, NEW JERSEY

Acknowledgment is made to the following publishers for permission to reprint copyrighted material:

Harcourt Brace Jovanovich, Inc., for lines from T. S. Eliot, "Choruses from *The Rock*" and "Ash Wednesday," in *Complete Poems and Plays*, 1909–1950, 1952.

Sheed & Ward, Inc., for prayers from Michel Quoist, *Prayers*, © Sheed & Ward, Inc., 1963.

The Viking Press, Inc., for lines from Siegfried Sassoon, "Everyone Sang," in *Collected Poems*, copyright 1948 by Siegfried Sassoon.

WHAT'S NEXT?

To our many young friends
who have contributed so much
to our understanding of Christian faith
active in love

CONTENTS

*The authors worked together closely on this book, sharing insights and suggestions. Ernest Gordon is primarily responsible for chapters 2, 3, 4, 8, 9, 10, 12, and 14; Peter Funk for overall planning and structuring and chapters 1, 5, 6, 7, 11, 13, and 15.

WHAT'S NEXT?

CHAPTER ONE

The New Christian

After some searching, we found the address.

It was an old, run-down apartment building a few blocks from Haight and Ashbury streets in San Francisco. In the sprawling entrance the one-time flower beds were overgrown with weeds, the empty pool in the center cracked and chipped.

We asked a young woman where we could find the Christian community.

"Third floor," she replied with some disdain. As we entered the building she called after us, laughing. "Better be careful! They may get *you.*"

It was a small community, perhaps ten people in all. Some of them sat on the floor talking. In a corner a girl and a young man were working a stencil machine. A few others were reading the Bible. In the kitchen a group was preparing a meal. From another room a radio played a current hit tune.

A young minister and his wife were staying there, helping to organize and to teach.

On a window seat were two youngsters, a girl and a boy who had been brought in off the streets the previous day. They were recovering from a bad drug trip and remained almost motionless. Occasionally the boy would murmur, "Praise God." He was aware that he was in kindly hands. From time to time someone would speak to them and they would return a tentative, trusting smile.

On the floor beside me was a large man in his early 20s. His black beard and curly hair had not been brushed. His eyes were feverish.

Having experienced conversion three weeks earlier, Frank was undergoing something of a crisis. Was it a dream? Was it simply an emotional trip? Now that the original feeling seemed to have diminished, what was left?

"How long have you been *saved?*" he almost shouted at me.

"What do you mean by *saved?*" I asked. I wanted to be sure we were talking about the same thing.

He floundered. "Known Jesus—How long have you known him?"

"Do you mean how long has it been since Jesus *saved* me from my fears, my worries, my unhappiness? How long that he's been my Lord, and that through him I'll have eternal life?"

Frank was under tension. He nodded. "Yeah."

"For a long while."

"Do you ever get to a point where—well, maybe you're wondering?"

"Sometimes. That's part of being human." We waited a bit. "You have a mother and father, don't you?"

"Everyone does." He was impatient.

"Whether you're at home, or here, or anywhere you're still their son. Right?"

He nodded, watching me carefully.

"Do you believe that Jesus was God's son, that he gave his life for us, for our sins?"

"Yes."

"And you believe he was resurrected, that God raised him from the dead?"

"I buy that."

I thumbed the pages of my Bible to Romans 10:9–13. "Because if you confess (that means to speak the words and mean them) with your lips that Jesus is Lord and believe in your heart that God raised him from the dead, you will be *saved.*

"For man believes with his heart and is so justified, and he confesses with his lips and is so saved. The Scripture says, 'No one who believes in him will be put to shame.' For there is no distinction between Jew and Greek; the same Lord is Lord of all and bestows his riches upon all who call upon him. For everyone who calls upon the name of the Lord will be saved."*

*Unless otherwise noted, Scripture is quoted from the Revised Standard Version.

He watched me, listening intently now.

"You've got to remember that what you believe, what you just agreed that you believe, is the most important thing that's happened to you," I said. "You believe in Jesus. You believe in his resurrection. That's *the* key to faith. From this your faith is going to grow. It's God's promise. It's not some magical gobbledygook. In this new birth you've had, the seed of God through Christ Jesus has been planted in you and you've been given a new life."

Since they were leaving to witness on the streets of San Francisco and Berkeley and I was returning to the East, I never saw Frank again. I have wondered what happened to him.

I had spoken with intense feeling, because this particular area once had been a stumbling block to me. Perhaps it was because while growing up, though I was instructed in Christianity, I was not given the expectation of having a direct experience with Christ. And it is Christ who dramatically and consistently changes and charges lives.

For most of us the experience of Frank has been, in one way or another, our own experience. We question. We doubt. We are cautiously optimistic or wistfully skeptical. Sometimes we are not sure what to believe or if there *is* anything to believe.

This is the reason that this guidebook, *What's Next?*, was written, for those new Christians who are unsure of the next steps in the Christian life. And for all those who want to know more about this faith and to deepen their experience.

The uncertainty of our beliefs reflects the uncertainty of our times. Older and traditional values are crumbling, society is shaped by technocrats, computers, misplaced values, and selfish desires. Even the Church seems to be caught up in confusion as it seeks answers. The prevailing culture often determines what the Christian or Jew will do and believe. Ministers, priests, and rabbis scramble frantically to be "relevant."

We are going through a period of agonizing change. Scientific breakthroughs are leading us into a new era. Whether we will be led into more of a hell than a paradise will depend on how we use our fantastic discoveries. It is certain, however, that we are at a critical juncture in history.

Perhaps *now*—at this crossroad more than at any previous time in history—is *the* hour of the Christian message. Perhaps here, at this particular point in time, the real purpose of Christianity is being made gloriously clear: God is summoning each of us in his own way, as followers of Jesus Christ, to help in leading mankind from the Wilderness.

God asks you to help him in two ways.

The first is this: whenever you find people who don't know much about the Gospel, and if you seem to have the opportunity, tell them about the good news, the best news mankind ever had. We are co-workers with God in his task of re-creating his world in the pattern of the new creation initiated in Jesus. Exactly how this will be done remains with God.

The second way to help God re-create his world is this: in your everyday work, in your secular position, live the Christian life and try to reshape the social framework around you.

It is in this reshaping that real change takes place, for the quality of life depends on underlying values. Superficial changes at the surface of life make little long-term difference. Influence the values and you influence life deeply. It is like digging a new river bed to change the direction of the flow of water.

To be able to do this, it is vital to understand what being a Christian means.

Anyone who knows history even a little is aware of the horrible deeds that have been done in the name of Christianity. But they are in name only, for no real Christian could commit those crimes. Whoever did them did not have a concept of the Christian way. We all know people who claim to be Christian, but do not act with the Christian spirit.

Frequently when one is converted and becomes a new Christian he thinks: "Wow! This is it! I've arrived! The journey's over!"

Actually, it's just begun.

In one sense we are all "new" Christians, for whether we are newly converted or "old" Christians we will continue to grow more into our faith. This is the beauty of our spiritual pilgrimage. It never ends. It is always fresh and new. God is always revealing himself to us in new ways, helping us to grow.

Each of us in our pilgrimage needs a spiritual guide. There are individual clergymen and laymen who have a depth of spirit and wisdom, but unfortunately they are not always available to those seeking guidance.

This guidebook for new Christians hopes to serve this purpose. It draws on a wide experience, going far beyond that of the authors. And it sets forth what being a Christian will mean in your life: the joys *and* the hazards. Sometimes people have the mistaken notion that being a Christian is like being a "goody-goody." They couldn't be more wrong. To be a Christian in today's world has much in common with what being a Christian was in the early centuries when most people were non-Christians. It is a tough job, but it is also where the real joy and beauty in life are to be found.

An intelligent, sensitive woman who has been a Christian since childhood commented to me in wonder: "I'm just beginning to understand what being a Christian involves. It is difficult because you can no longer look at the world in the same old way. And I never realized the tremendous discipline it took—to search out your pride, control your anger, to practice love consistently, to get rid of envy and greed, to control your appetites and to fulfill your responsibilities even when you don't feel like it."

It is tempting to criticize and to find fault with the Church today. What critics don't grasp is that the Church is trying to cope with all the ills besetting mankind. The Church is not some disembodied, legal institution. The Church is people. The bewilderment of people is reflected in the Church's outward appearance. But equally the Church is the deep reflection of Christ and as such will meet the demands of the changing times.

Within the organized Church itself some of the changes can be seen in the modified liturgy, in the forms of worship, the music, the more casual dress of worshipers, in the growing importance of laymen. Ballet and plays are used to reinforce the Gospel message with dramatic effect.

I attended a rock festival that was entirely religious. The new music was compelling. Some of the bands were booked also in night clubs in the cities, giving the musicians a chance to do some subtle witnessing.

The outward form of the Church in the future undoubtedly will be different. New and better ways of communicating the Gospel and of creating a sense of community will be found. But the central message of Christ is unchangeable. It is for all men at all times.

People are painfully aware of the failure of the strictly secular approach to solving society's problems. Because they are inherently religious beings they search for answers beyond themselves.

Some turn to astrology and offbeat occult experiments. In the long run, however, these esoteric teachings do not hold up. They only lead to the self, and the self cannot save the self.

Throughout the cycle of history, religious revivals have recurred similar to what we are experiencing today when many people are turning to Jesus. The results of these revivals are usually positive. The Church is jolted into a renewed understanding of its mission.

The rediscovery of Jesus brings with it a vision of life as it can be lived. It embodies the longing for a simpler, more honest life, for the restoration of the dignity of man as an individual, for the hope that man will find beauty in all that God has made. It is saying to the world that men can live together tolerantly and in peace. And it is showing this not in words, but in deeds.

If you are a "new" Christian, if you are an uncertain Christian, this book will give you the essence of what Christianity is all about—and once having that essence, how you may practice it for the benefit of God, of others, of yourself.

> Here I am, Lord;
> Here is my body,
> Here is my heart,
> Here is my soul.
> Grant that I may be big enough to reach the world.
> Strong enough to carry it,
> Pure enough to embrace it without wanting to keep it.
> Grant that I may be a meeting-place, but a temporary one,
> A road that does not end in itself, because everything to be gathered there, everything human, leads toward you.*

*Michel Quoist, *Prayers* (New York: Sheed & Ward, 1963).

CHAPTER TWO

The Newness of Jesus

Jesus is *new*.

He is not a myth, not merely a kind of superprophet who lived 2000 years ago.

Jesus *is*. Jesus is *now*. Because he is *now* he is *new*.

He is radically new. He is uniquely new. He is newer to our age than atomic energy because his newness is *now*. It is of this moment even as you read these words. He is new because nothing like Jesus has ever happened before in the world.

He is new because when you encounter Jesus your life changes. Yet in an astonishing sense your life changes in a manner that your deepest self has yearned for all along. He is new because if enough people would let Jesus work through them, if they opened their lives to his power, the world would be revolutionized. There would be peace, and the misery of the suffering would be alleviated.

To comprehend fully the newness of Jesus today, we should understand the startling newness of him in his own time.

The scribes (lawyers), priests, and Pharisees formed the most powerful group in Palestine, for they believed that only they were capable of interpreting God's word.

Then Jesus arrived, claiming that he was God's son, that only by following him could people enter the Kingdom of Heaven. He was the fulfillment of God's promise to send a Messiah.

The leading Jews of Israel were shocked and horrified that anyone would make such blasphemous claims.

Jesus replied to their attacks: "I have shown you many good works from the Father; for which of these do you stone me?' The Jews answered him, 'We stone you for no good work but for blasphemy; because you, being a man, make yourself God' " (John 10: 32–33).

Yet, thousands flocked to him because what Jesus said was so radically new and exciting, and the life-style he urged was so completely different. They sensed he had hold of the truth.

Our own times have many similarities. We too have our Pharisees and scribes, men who solemnly pronounce that it is only through science that man can be saved, or sociologists who believe that most problems will be rectified by changing environments and governmental systems. We have politicians, college administrators, and economists who offer innumerable panaceas. But they all miss an obvious answer. Jesus said the evil in the world comes out of the hearts of men, and until there is an "inner" revolution, there is no lasting hope for mankind.

When someone comes to you stating certain facts, you want to know his credentials. In the same way, you want to know the "authority" of Jesus Christ.

1. He Is the New Authority

As we read the Bible we begin to see how God has a purpose for his world and his people. That is why he created the cosmos, chose Abraham, Isaac, and Jacob, and called their children to be his witnesses. He liberated them from the slavery of Egypt, disciplined them in the wilderness of Sinai, spoke his word through the prophets, and gave them his Law to guide them. When they failed God because of their contentious stubbornness he took action, magnificent action. He "sent forth his Son, born of a woman, born into the law, to redeem those who were under the law, so that we might receive adoption as sons" (Gal. 4:4).

The experience of Jesus today is the same kind of experience known by the first disciples, for it is the same person.

Those who knew him in the flesh either turned to him or away from him. There is no neutrality with respect to Jesus. If you are not for him then by implication you are against him. Those who followed him were led into a new experience of life. They learned from him as a man. They witnessed the authority of his teaching as one who had come from God (John 3:2). They saw his message in himself *as* the messenger.

They saw God manifested in Jesus. The blind received sight, the crippled walked, people were liberated from the law of the scribes, undesirables were loved, despised tax collectors were respected, prostitutes and junkies were given a new chance. The healing and the saving power of God was seen at work.

One day on the way to Jerusalem, Jesus asked his followers what men thought of him. He was told that some men thought he was John the Baptist, others Elijah, Jeremiah, or one of the other prophets.

Then he asked them what they thought. Peter replied as the spokesman: "You are the Christ, the son of the living God."

Having been with him, they knew. When you encounter Jesus on a personal level, you too will know the same thing.

The disciples followed him first as an extraordinary man, one who was at least a prophet. But they learned by their experience that in fact God was with them.

It is through Jesus that God speaks to his world, all of it. To speak as he did, God chose to limit himself to a man living in a particular place at a particular time with particular friends. By this action God fulfilled what he promised in the Old Testament.

Some people say that there is nothing new about the Christian faith. It has all been said before by teachers of various religions. But, like the first disciples, we can only reply that the newness of Christianity is the newness of Jesus.

The evidence of this is summed up in the following characteristics of Jesus' life.

He is the new authority who speaks for God to all mankind. People who witnessed his miracles and heard his words were amazed.

"By what authority does he do these things?"

For years the Jews had heard scholars answer their questions with such uncertainty and with so many vague, equivocating references that they were left more bewildered than ever. Jesus, on the other hand, spoke directly to their needs. He had no reason to refer to the authorities. He was and is *the* authority. He speaks the new word to man because he is *the word.* As a consequence his words sparkle with freshness.

When the Law was read it was customary for those who listened to respond at the conclusion of each passage with the words: *amen, amen,* or *verily, verily,* or *truly, truly.* This is another way of saying "let it happen."

But when Jesus spoke it was different. He spoke with the *Amen* of God. That is, he prefixed his discourses with "Amen, Amen," or would begin "I say to you." The words from his lips were those of God. In him the *Word* of God was happening. The activity of God was visible in personal terms. This is indeed exactly what Jesus said to Nicodemus in the closing remarks of his discussion with him: "The Father loves the son, and has given all things [or all authority] into his hand" (John 3:35).

2. He Is the Liberator

Because of our limitations as human beings, we cannot help but commit wrongs against God and our neighbor. The Good News of Jesus is that through him we are liberated from the control and power of our sins. It is because of this that he has the power to heal our minds and bodies when we turn to him in prayer.

His first visit to Nazareth at the beginning of his ministry was a dramatic event, for it was actually his announcement to the world of his mission.

He worshiped in the synagogue as usual. Since it was his native town his neighbors were undoubtedly glad to see him. Then he took the scrolls and read from Isaiah 61: "The Spirit of the Lord God is upon me, because the Lord has anointed me to bring good tidings to the afflicted; he has sent me to bind up the broken-hearted, to proclaim liberty to the captives, and the opening of the prison to those who are bound . . . to comfort all who mourn."

As he looked out over the congregation he stated that this prophecy was now being fulfilled in him.

They were furious at his presumption, and he was thrown out of his native town. The rest of Jesus' life was much like that, for "he came to his own home, and his own people received him not" (John 1:11).

The forgiveness given by Jesus is no cheap thing. It involves his confrontation with the powers of evil disguised as good. His struggle with those destructive forces, and his death upon the cross—the death that overcame death and the ultimate power of sin—is the struggle of God for us. Its end is victoriously proclaimed from the cross by the words: "It is finished," and is seen visibly by the triumph of the resurrection.

3. The Sabbath Is for Freedom

Jesus further demonstrated his divine authority by claiming to be Lord of the Sabbath. This day had been set aside by God as holy for man. One day in the week he was free from the controls of the ruler, boss, society, and law. He was free to worship God and experience the reality of freedom in his relationship with the creator.

Because of human stupidity, this divine law for human freedom had been reduced to an enslaving rule. Rather than being able to relax, people were still under the burden of niggling rules and regulations.

Jesus claimed the freedom of the Sabbath by healing in it. He understood God's intent for this holy day. This too was held in evidence against him. His reply to such condemnation was ringingly clear: "The sabbath was made for man, not man for the sabbath; so the Son of man is lord even of the sabbath" (Mark 2:27–28). We may regard this statement as the guage of Jesus' authority. Since it is *of* God, it is *for* man.

4. The Uniqueness of His Words

When he was concluding his Sermon on the Mount he said: "Every one then who hears these words of mine and does them will be like a wise man who built his house upon the rock" (Matt. 7:24).

We may test the uniqueness of these words for ourselves by studying the uniqueness of Jesus' teaching. He turns the values of everyday acceptance upside down and presents us with the command that only God can make.

The Sermon on the Mount, for example, is so different from the way we live that many of us ignore it gladly, or else shrug our shoulders to say: "There's nothing we can do about it. It is an impossible ethic. It's all right in theory, or for a saint, but too much for the ordinary man."

Such a conclusion is wrong, for Jesus' teaching is for all people everywhere in every age.

In a religion that is concerned only with laws and abstract theories the individual may seem alone in a cold universe. Because of Jesus all this is changed. He brings us directly and personally into the presence of our God, who welcomes us in love. At times we may be almost overwhelmed by this experience, for he loves all of us as though there were only one of us to love.

The kind of love Jesus shows leads us to "faith." For too long churchmen have interpreted faith as the right belief which is found in doctrines established by ecclesiastical councils or committees. Such a meaning is too tiny to hold the bigness of faith that Jesus lived and taught. The faith he introduces us to is that which moves mountains, heals the sick, raises the dead—as well as a bit of "hell" at times— casts out demons, speaks in new tongues, and affirms the presence of God.

Faith is not the creation of our own imagination, but our response to God's initiative. Paul Tillich writes of it as "the courage to be." It is the experience of being "grasped by the power of being."

To be grasped implies a personal encounter. When someone grasps me I invariably turn toward her or him. Faith is just this: a turning to our Father who "grabs" by his loving actions shown through Jesus.

The revolutionary character of Jesus and his works are summed up in his proclamation of the rule of God, or the reign of God, or the Kingdom of God. The radical newness of this is clearly expressed by Mark: "Now after John was arrested, Jesus came into Galilee preaching the gospel of God, and saying, 'The time is fulfilled, and the kingdom of God is at hand; repent, and believe in the gospel' " (Mark 1:14–15).

His bold words shocked and frightened many, but God's hour had struck. In Jesus his word was spoken, calling men to commit themselves to the divine way of life, to obeying his will, and to the discipleship of Jesus Christ his son.

Whereas the Jews looked toward the restoration of th
empire under a military Messiah, Jesus revealed that the ru
is not according to this world. It is obedience, passionate obedience
to the commands spoken by Jesus. It calls for complete commitment.
By this commitment our consciousness is intensified to the extent that
we know with certitude that we are in the divine presence.

In this presence our lives are renewed and completed. We have
become kinsmen by faith with Jesus. We are claimed by God as his
own. What we have to do is to respond. Like the prodigal son, we may
say, "Father, I have sinned against heaven and before you; I am no
longer worthy to be called your son" (Luke 15:21).

Living in the *presence* obviously implies a new standard as well as
a new quality of life. Our ultimate loyalty must be for God and God
alone. No one else is worthy of it. To be in the Kingdom of God is
to surrender all our other loyalties and to be obedient to his will.

5. The Resurrection

What we have said so far is important only in the light of
the newest and most radical of all events: the resurrection of Jesus.

He died and was buried. But he was raised from the dead on the
third day. God did it.

The Father raised his Son. Death is overcome. Life is assured to all
who follow him. The crucifixion and the resurrection are part of the
same divine action. In 1 Corinthians 15, Paul points out that as
descendents of the first Adam we are heirs of death. But because of
Jesus Christ, the new Adam, "all shall be made alive." Jesus has
pioneered a way through the ultimate prison wall for man and has
opened the way to eternal life.

When Jesus was raised from the dead and "ascended to God" he
was to be with all his people at all times. He was known in Galilee
and in Jerusalem. He was known by the disciples in the upper room,
and by two of them on the road to Emmaus. He was known by Paul
on the way to Damascus. He was and is known by millions of people
who have never seen him, and yet believe (see John 20:29).

The same Jesus who was crucified is the one who is "alive for
evermore" (Rev. 1:18).

In *Jesus Rediscovered*, Malcolm Muggeridge, a one-time optimistic rationalist who became an optimistic Christian, affirms that "you can derive strength and illumination from the man in the Gospels which you cannot achieve, we'll say for instance, with Socrates who was a very wise and good man who also died."*

He is alive.

Because he is, he grasps us where we are and as we are. On this foundation is built the New Covenant and the community of Christian faith. The power of God that was in Jesus, and that raised him from the dead, continues through the resurrection to bring us into fellowship with him. The power that does this is the Holy Spirit. Jesus has promised to live with those who love him, and to have the Holy Spirit instruct us in his truth.

"If a man loves me, he will keep my word, and my Father will love him, and we will come to him and make our home with him. . . .These things I have spoken to you, while I am still with you. But the Counselor, the Holy Spirit, whom the Father will send in my name, he will teach you all things, and bring to your remembrance all that I have said to you (John 14:23–26; see also John 16:12–15).

The same word that was spoken to his disciples is spoken to us today. By loving Jesus we continue to know more about him in a growing friendship. Our commitment to him is continuous. It is following him, seeing people with his eyes, walking with him along a road that leads through death to life. We are sharers now in his resurrection. "Whoever lives and believes in me shall never die (John 11:26).

In an encounter with Jesus we are experiencing ultimate reality. Too much of contemporary religious thought pays attention to the importance of religious experience without concerning itself with the object of experience: Christ. The experience many people have, as a consequence, is centered upon the self. The self cannot save itself.

I was called in by a nineteen-year-old boy recently who had been on a long and bad LSD trip. What frightened him enormously was his sense of being in a black void, the ultimate in despair. It was hell. When we center our experience upon ourselves and search for reality

---

Jesus Rediscovered (Garden City, N.Y.: Doubleday, 1969).

within ourselves, we'll find what the young man who had taken the wrong way found, namely the abyss of nothingness.

The experience of the living Christ is radically different.

It brings us into the full stream of God's life, face to face with the Eternal who has the human face of Jesus.

CHAPTER THREE

What Happens When You Are Converted?

You turn to God!

This means turning from what?

From the world, the flesh, and the devil according to the *Book of Common Prayer.* This trinity of evil has an awesome sound to it. But we know it well. It is what separates us from each other, and cuts us off from God.

Consider the three temptations of Jesus as they are recorded by Matthew and Luke and touched upon by Mark. Jesus is not tempted to perform what we would call evil. He was tempted to do something that wasn't good enough.

His people believed that when the Messiah came he would prepare an enormous banquet to indicate that the day of the Lord had come. Jesus refused to turn stones into bread. It was not by bread alone that men lived, but by the word of God.

They believed that he would have supernatural power great enough to escape any harm his enemies might try to do to him. And so he was tempted to show that he had such power. But Jesus, again quoting from Scripture, pointed out that it was evil to test God in this way.

He was tempted to respond to the nationalistic expectations of his people, and seize the power of Caesar to reign as one greater than King David. All that was asked of him was homage to Satan. But Jesus said, "Begone Satan! Scripture says, 'You shall do homage to the Lord your God and worship him alone' " (Matt. 4:10, NEB).

To Jesus' contemporaries those temptations were not evil but good. But Jesus showed them that they were not good enough. What is good enough for men and societies is not good enough for God.

We must turn away from all that is not good enough. Where do we begin? With ourselves! According to society, we may be reckoned to be good if we are successful at school and business, if we are not caught breaking the law, if we pay our taxes and give to charity. The goodness required of us by God is much more than this.

It was this kind of inadequate goodness a young man truly believed in when he came to Jesus asking for eternal life. Jesus understood him fully, and challenged him to turn to the ultimate goodness of God. "You lack one thing; go, sell what you have, and give to the poor, and you will have treasure in heaven; come, and follow me" (Mark 10:17–21).

That was a hard demand. It has to be understood in terms of the man's request. He wanted the ultimate good he called "eternal life." How great was his need, and how sincere his quest? Not great enough nor sincere enough. Sorrowfully, he turned back to the demands of the lesser good. And Jesus agonized for him because he loved him.

In his own way each one of us must face the ultimate demand of God. He does not have to agree to our terms, but we do have to agree to his. God demands only the best.

Even if we realize that the commonly accepted values of our society are not good enough, we are still left to face the fact that neither are we. Sometimes it takes a crisis or a judgment to make us aware of this. We may have criticized our parents, our spouses, our friends, our teachers, our government, our associates, our pastors for their lack of goodness without criticizing ourselves.

If we are to be honest, however, we are bound to confess at some time or another that *we* are not good enough. We cannot do the good that we know we ought to do, and instead do the evil we do not want to do (see Rom. 7:19).

One by one, as we learn to evaluate ourselves, our times, and our societies, we are left to join the tax collector in his prayers, "Lord have mercy on me, a sinner."

One night as I was preparing for bed, the doorbell rang. I opened it to an undergraduate who had come to see me as the last port of call.

The student was facing the crisis of his human failure. Superficially he was a success. He was a university scholar in the top ten of his class.

His parents were wealthy. He was politically active with a group that believed strongly in the divinity of dollars. He had been brought up to believe that he could do anything he wanted. He was on the way to achieving what he had been taught to want. But there was a flaw: himself! What he had discovered himself to be was too much. He tried to commit suicide by jumping over a bridge into a river. His ability as a swimmer, however, prevented him from fulfilling his intention. He was left with himself and the problem of what he wanted not being good enough.

His story, though in a different form, is the story of mankind. What we are as individuals and what we are collectively is not nearly good enough. We cannot go it alone or do it ourselves.

This lack of goodness is anything but passive. It is active; destructively active. Because we are not good enough we have contributed to the downfall of the world. We have destroyed millions of fellow human beings in wars that have so often been justified in highly righteous terms, in innumerable acts that demonstrate agonizingly the horror of "man's inhumanity to man," in attitudes and relationships that have broken people's hearts and ruined their lives. The tragic truth we learn slowly is that the only original thing we give to the world is our own original sin.

In the human situation of man without God our lot is hopeless. What we are and what we do can never save us from the grim, inexorable end of the law of sin, namely, the final destruction of death.

From the reality of sin as it affects me I can learn that my own consciousness of sin cannot be explained adequately in terms of the natural and social orders alone. Somehow or other I am dimly aware as a moral person of having fallen from a greater goodness, and at the same time I am also aware that I aspire to it.

In the magnificent parable of the prodigal son (Luke 15:11–32), the prodigal cut himself off from home by demanding his inheritance and going off to live in the "wasteland." There he was, a social success until his money ran out; then he became a failure, such a failure that he suffered the worst possible fate for a Jew: He became a swineherd. He had reached rock bottom. In his human extremity he realized that his father's square ways were infinitely better than anything he had experienced in Sin City. He couldn't go back as a son. Legally he had denied and rejected this relationship. He could, however, be a servant, and he turned to that role when he realized that the pigsty wasn't good enough. Because of his need he took the homeward trail. It was the expedient thing to do.

In Conversion We Turn to God

We turn from ourselves and our sinful ways to God. Our intellects and environments cannot give us an adequate answer. The only explanation of our moral experience must be beyond it. This is the explanation given by Jesus to the man seeking eternal life: "No one is good but God alone" (Mark 10:18).

In turning to God, however, we must be ruthlessly honest with ourselves so that we do not create an idol in our own image. Since time immemorial men and women have turned to the state, to society's code of conduct, to the stars, to reason, to drugs or alcohol, to humanity in essence, and called it God. But God is *not* of our creation.

The Greeks in their day taught that there was an impersonal moral law operating within the universe. To go against this law was to become the victim of fate. Noble men such as Oedipus were brought by their fate to a tragic and destructive end. Many people have believed in a god like this. It is not surely to this we are asked to turn; for this is none other than what Paul classified as "the power of sin" (Rom. 3:9). He goes on to show that God has gone beyond the law of fate and the moral law to reveal his justice. By this justice the victims of law "are justified by his [God's] grace as a gift, through the redemption which is in Christ Jesus" (Rom. 3:24).

In the light of biblical evidence we are bound to take another look at what the word "God" means to us. As a word it denotes that to which we give our ultimate loyalty. The Bible, however, tells us of the God to whom we are to be completely faithful.

He is the God who liberates. In the revelation received by Moses at the giving of the Law, God said, "I am the Lord your God, who brought you out of the land of Egypt, out of the house of bondage." (Exod. 20:2, Deut. 5:6). He is for our freedom; he sets us free. The black people of this country know this truth better than most of the whites. They have expressed their trust in the liberating work of God in the words of the spiritual:

> Thus saith the Lord, bold Moses said,
> Let my people go.
> If not I'll smite your first-born dead,
> Let my people go.

God liberates his people because he loves them. Without his love there can be no authentic freedom. There may be substitutes such as being free to do my own thing, or free to please myself, or free to make as much as I can, or free to dominate others, or free to deny God. Such apparent freedom is, in the end, enslaving and destructive. History has countless examples. When we are liberated, however, by God's love, we are set free from the controls of our fears, hates, anxieties, prejudices, and also from the power of sin, death, and society. We are set free by love to love, even those who claim to be our enemies. "For God sent the Son into the world, not to condemn the world, but that the world might be *saved* through him" (John 3:17). Instead of "saved" we could use "liberated," for to be "saved" is to be set free.

Let us return to the experience of the prodigal son, for it is the supreme example of conversion. The prodigal returned home because he knew that he would be better off there than in Sin City. He expected to be received as a hired hand and put to work to take care of the corn and the animals. His father, however, had forgotten about the law his son had claimed when he renounced his right of sonship. He was out looking for him. When he saw him trudging along the long trail he rushed out to greet him. Think of what the sight must have meant to the prodigal. There is his father running to him, not with a whip in his hand, but with his arms outstretched to embrace. Before he knows what is happening to him, he is being hugged and kissed.

Most of us have a good memory like this to guide our own thoughts.

I lived on a rocky point that jutted out as the long arm of a deep ocean bay. I had a girl friend I wanted to visit. My choice was to row across three miles of the ocean or walk seven miles by land.

I rowed.

On my way back a storm blew up. The wind was against me. I was within sight of the point. I was also at the end of my physical resources. Turning around I looked. There was Dad standing on the point waiting. When I fought my way near to it, Dad waded out to grasp my boat and prevent it from being overturned by the waves lashing against the rocks. Through that action my father revealed himself to me. I realized that it was I who did not understand him rather than the other way around.

An English poet sums up the Christian experience in two lines:

> What is conversion but turning round,
> To look upon a love profound.

Love profound does not exist in a vacuum or as an abstraction. It is the activity of God the Father. We see that activity superbly in Jesus who died for us while we were yet sinners.

When I was staying at a luxurious hotel, I flipped through the Gideon Bible by my bedside. In the third chapter of John's Gospel I noted that the sixteenth verse was heavily underlined. At the bottom of the page was a footnote: "To think God loves a down-and-outer like me so much!"

Obviously the man or woman who had written these words wasn't a social or economic dropout. He had turned round "to look upon a love profound." Having done so he had taken the measure of himself.

Conversion to God, therefore, involves us in a quality of life that is gloriously different from anything that can be found in the prodigal's Sin City. The laws and attitudes of godless people condemn us for our very humanity; for not being a cog in the machinery of the state. But God's love in Christ reaches out to save, liberate, and exalt.

As a soldier in a Highland Regiment I was at war for six years of active service that included tragic battles, wounds, and imprisonment. I became accustomed to fear, hate, brutality, torture, and despair. I lost my fear of pain and death and of what other men could do to me. I was hardened by the laws of nations and the experience of existence. Death and hell could not scare me. What changed my life was the experience of "love profound" as I saw it active in the lives of converted men. They showed me the way to "love profound": to Jesus, the activity of the Father.

The Nature and When of Conversion

The nature of our conversion is not determined by ourselves or by a particular group of religious people. It is the activity of God. Theologians in the past called it *prevenient grace.* What it means is that God grasps us in such a way that we are compelled to respond.

When we admit the divine initiative as the beginning of conversion, we are free to see the greatness of its nature and range. It is not only up to us. The mystery is, we know along with Paul, that we "are called according to his [God's] purpose" (Rom. 8:28).

To be aware that we are within God's purpose is to rejoice that conversion has happened and is happening in our lives.

For some the experience comes like a flash of light, as it did to Saul on the way to Damascus. It may be highly dramatic in its nature, as it has been for many prisoners, alcoholics, junkies—"tax collectors." This doesn't exclude housewives, children, students, and all people in their everyday walks of life.

I heard one of the Jesus people in Los Angeles give her testimony over the radio. She was a pretty girl who had gone to Hollywood hoping to achieve a career in films. A man assured her that he was a producer who would soon get her a major part in one of his productions. In exchange for this promised favor she slept with him. He introduced her to drugs. When she was under their influence he sold her lovely body to several men each day. In moments of relative sanity she was horrified at what she was doing. She was bitter with shame and shocked with fright.

One day she stumbled into a Christian coffeehouse, where a group of Jesus people understood her plight. They took her with them to a house in which they lived as a community of faith. They stood by her as she dried out, singing hymns and praying as she screamed in the agony of withdrawal. At the depth of her suffering she suddenly had a wonderful sense of peace and love. Jesus, she felt, was by her side. She believed in him. From then on she recovered quickly and knew beyond doubt that her moment with Jesus was the moment of her conversion.

Some people know that they have been with Jesus all their lives. Once, on a bicycle tour of the Scottish Highlands, I was invited in for a meal of kid stew by an old lady, the widow of a Free Church minister. She was sweet and gentle. During our conversation she told me that her life had been full of blessings, but the greatest one of all was knowing the Lord Jesus. She had grown up knowing him and could not remember a time when it was otherwise.

Some discover that they were Christians before they were aware of it. An acquaintance of mine was an active Communist and self-styled atheist during his college days. Years afterward a friend saw him coming out of a morning worship service. He asked him: "Andrew, I didn't know you were a Christian?" He replied: "To tell you the truth, I didn't know myself until a few months ago. But now I do."

Some struggle intellectually for years before they are certain of their conversion. W. H. Auden, Malcolm Muggeridge, and C. E. M. Joad are a few of those. In America I have known distinguished men and women who have struggled hard to come by their faith.

C. S. Lewis's autobiography, *Surprised by Joy,* is a series of three incidents that made him aware of the supernatural dimension. Eventually he was led, struggling, into the presence of God to find that he was not an idea, not a formula, not an abstraction, but the Person, the Eternal—*I am.*

Conversion may be slow or sudden, gradual or dramatic. There is no rigid pattern. The activity of the Holy Spirit is not limited to any single way. God is too big for any of our small formulas.

Though conversion may come at *any* age, the majority of them take place in youth. The first twelve disciples were young men. John was probably a teen-ager, the boy of the group, beloved by Jesus.

But as the Holy Spirit is not limited by method, so is he not limited by age. Luke tells us of Simeon, a man of many years presumably, who had been told by the Holy Spirit that he would not die until he saw "the Lord's Christ." When he saw him in the Temple, he sang his hymn of conversion:

> Now, Lord, you have kept your promise,
> and you may let your servant go in peace.
> For with my own eyes I have seen your salvation,
> Which you have made ready in the presence of all peoples:

> A light to reveal your way to the Gentiles,
> And to give glory to your people Israel.
> (Luke 2:29–32, *Good News for Modern Man*)

Conversion has its antecedents. The moment of illumination or awareness is preceded by other moments when God addressed us and we did not recognize it. Stephen, one of the original seven deacons, made a splendid witness for his Lord before the council of Jerusalem. He was thrown out of the city and stoned to death. The style of his dying was as splendid as his spoken testimony. His last words were a repetition of his Lord's: "Do not hold this sin against them."

A young man witnessed this execution. His name was Saul. His immediate reaction was to increase his hostility toward Christ's followers. He destroyed the church and dragged men and women off to prison. He was so zealous in persecuting Jesus' people that he requested permission from the high priest to purge the synagogues of Damascus of those who belonged "to the Way."

On the journey to Damascus he met the Lord in a dramatic confrontation in which he was blinded. At the same time he was "born again." The Lord sent to him the Christian Ananias, who said: "Brother Saul, receive your sight." And in receiving his sight, in a very real sense he was given new vision. He was baptized and witnessed in the synagogue, proclaiming Jesus as the Son of God.

The witness of faithful Stephen made a tremendous impact on proud, young Saul. He was touched by God's gracious action, but he rebelled against it.

No one may determine exactly where his or her conversion takes place. To do so may be to become guilty of spiritual pride, by far the worst kind. What matters is the reality of turning to God. Paul has the right word: "I planted, Apollos watered, but God gave the growth. So neither he who plants nor he who waters is anything, but only God who gives the growth" (1 Cor. 3:6–7).

Although Paul stepped immediately into the role of an apostle, "as one born out of due season," he confesses not only that he had to grow from childhood to maturity, but that he was still at the beginning of eternal truth: "When I became a man, I gave up childish ways. For now we see in a mirror dimly, but then face to face" (1 Cor. 13:11–12).

Going on to the "face to face" encounter means being converted more and more from the world and its ways and converted more to be in Christ and to become like him. In the Bible there is only the record of one man who is perfect as God is perfect. The condition of the converted person is that he is saved, is being saved, and will be saved.

We are dependent upon God and the working of the Holy Spirit for our conversion. We are also dependent upon the witness of others. There is always someone to introduce us to our Lord.

For two years a student visited me regularly in order to argue angrily why he didn't like me, my work, or the Good News I declared.

Several years after he had graduated I received a telegram from him: "Converted at last. Thank you. You pointed the way."

Conversion—when, how, and through whom it comes is God's business from first to last. It results in a new relationship with him, and through him, with each other. In this relationship, Christ is always at the center, and beside him are our brothers and sisters for whom he died. We cannot love him without loving them at the same time. In loving them we find that by them we are greatly beloved.

The moment of conversion, therefore, is not marked by a point or a full stop but by a triangle: God, my brothers, and myself.

By turning to God through Jesus Christ we find that we turn to others, who like ourselves have turned from the world and its not-good-enough ways. These others may not be according to our choice or liking. They are chosen by God, not by us.

CHAPTER FOUR

What Does God Expect of You?

There can be only one answer: *All of you!*

This answer is not as simple as it may seem at first sight. What we are is so broken up and divided by many loyalties that it is hard to give our whole selves to God. We are loyal to our home, our school, our neighborhood, our friends, our race, our political party, our country, our prejudices. What we are, therefore, is spread out in bits and pieces. Thus we often find ourselves in conflict because one loyalty is challenging and competing with another.

Our loyalty to our business is in conflict with our loyalty to our home. Our boss wants us to work until eight. Dinner is waiting for us at seven. If we don't work until eight, we're in trouble. If we don't arrive at the table by seven, we're in trouble. We are loyal to our school, and we have a paper to write for tomorrow, but we are loyal to our friends who have invited us to a party. Papers and parties don't go well together so we are in a quandary.

God doesn't ask us for part of our loyalty. He is not one among others to whom we distribute a favor as we see fit. He asks for our whole self, our complete and utter loyalty.

He expects to be first in our lives. Jesus has demonstrated this to the full. He was obedient even to the extent of dying on the cross. That was not easy. In the garden of Gethsemane he prayed to be relieved of the coming agony. Yet in obedience he completed his prayer: "Thy will, not mine, be done."

When his family heard that Jesus' teaching had been upsetting the dignitaries, they came to fetch him home. Hearing of their purpose, he stretched out his arms to embrace the crowd listening to him and said, "Here are my mother and my brothers! Whoever does the will of God is my brother, and sister, and mother" (Mark 3:34–35). Nothing could equal the loyalty expected by God.

In turn, Jesus expected the same quality of loyalty from his disciples. These words of his may seem harsh: "If any one comes to me and does not hate his own father and mother and wife and children and brothers and sisters, yes, and even his own life, he cannot be my disciple" (Luke 14:26).

Jesus does not mean we are to dislike our family. He meant that unequivocally God is first in all things. There are no halfway measures. It is all or nothing. If the words upset us, it may be because of the absolute demand they make of us. We may be willing to give a part of ourselves, the part that is left over when we've given away the rest of ourselves to many things, causes, and interests. But a part is never enough.

In our highest moments of experience we are conscious of ourselves, conscious of being conscious; but more than that, we are sometimes conscious of a moral challenge or demand that is different from and greater than anything we have learned at home or school. This command has the quality of "you shall" about it. It is a moral imperative experienced in the most personal way.

Usually you conform to the moral standard of peers and society, but occasionally you may step out of these limiting patterns of action. You may be running for a train with only a few seconds left to catch it. If you don't you will be in trouble, for the next train will not get you to your job on time. The girl running ahead of you has caught her heel in a cracked pavement. As she falls, she cries in pain.

The sensible thing to do is to keep running. You don't. You stop. You think she has probably broken an ankle. You call the police and ask for an ambulance. By the time it comes, the next train has gone. When you arrive at work, you are told your services are no longer required. Anyone who cannot arrive in time obviously has no interest in the good of the firm; therefore, he does not merit its employ. You curse the firm, kick yourself, and wonder why you did such a stupid thing as to help a female with high heels who probably deserved her fall, and anyway, someone else could have helped her. Despite the back room quarterbacking you may indulge in, you are left with the confidence that what you did was right. Why it was right you are uncertain. All you know is that you responded to a demand greater than that of everyday standards.

This is what Pascal conceived of as the glory of man in the midst of his misery. Man is not a hunk of raw material to be manipulated. He responds to a higher call.

Our experiences of a response to a "distant drummer" are best understood in terms of the Bible's wisdom. The uniqueness of creation is that man became "a living soul," a conscious being, one who is aware of God's activity and who has the freedom to reply in his own way.

Through the agency of Moses, the Israelites were liberated from the slave stockades of Egypt. For a generation they were disciplined in the wilderness of Sinai until they became more and more conscious of the word God spoke to them. The peak point of that experience is the giving of the Ten Commandments.

The God of freedom gave the Decalogue as the moral guide for his people. It is the expression of his moral demand. These commandments are not as negative as we may have been taught to believe. The first four tell us of our response to God. The least he expects of us is our complete loyalty. We cannot worship idols and him at the same time, nor create a likeness of ourselves and call it God. By honoring him as the Lord of our life we will not take his name in vain by doing anything unworthy of him.

By remembering the Sabbath and respecting it as a gift for our freedom we shall endeavor to uphold the freedom of others to worship our Father and to reverence the holiness of all life.

Through our response to God we are liberated to care for our neighbors and their needs. These other six commandments respect the dignity and integrity of others.

The commandments are summed up in two texts, one from Deuteronomy, the other from Leviticus. "You shall love the Lord your God with all your heart, and with all your soul, and with all your strength, and with all your mind; and your neighbor as yourself" (Luke 10:27). The practical implications of the divine expectation are obvious. We are called to choose God and life and to find our fulfillment in the community of his love. Once again we are brought face to face with the truth that the truly personal life is the one that is lived in our relationship with God and our fellows.

I cannot love God without loving my neighbor. I cannot love my neighbor unless I also love myself. I cannot love myself without loving God. This is the everlasting triangle of life. It is beautifully summed up in the first letter of John: "We love, because he first loved us. If any one says, 'I love God,' and hates his brother, he is a liar; for he who does not love his brother whom he has seen, cannot love God whom he has not seen. And this commandment we have from him, that he who loves God should love his brother also" (1 John 4:19–21).

The Bible constantly upsets the prejudices of privilege that pass for morality in most societies. If you think God expects nothing from us but a few kind words spoken from our easy chairs, forget your intention of being a Christian. You've turned to the wrong demand. Try something else. A cross was good enough for God's Son. Why should you expect something less?

Another summing up of God's expectation is to be found in the teaching of Micah, the prophet. In the sixth chapter he tells his people of God's actions and asks them why they have become weary of him. He liberated them from slavery and cared for them in every phase of their history. By his saving acts he has shown the Israelites his nature. Having done so, he cannot accept bribes or crumbs from a rich man's table. The prophet goes on to describe what God expects: "He has showed you, O man, what is good; and what does the Lord require of you but to do justice, and to love kindness, and to walk humbly with your God" (Mic. 6:8). Here is the eternal triangle!

God expects us *to do justice.* Often societies have made the mistake of thinking that justice is in their moral codes and national laws. Leaving it there in the security of oblivion, they have gone about the task of doing their own thing in their own way without reference to God or anyone else. But justice in the prophet's sense is *morality in action.* It is doing what you believe and say is right.

To love kindness. The best interpretation of this is a phrase from a prayer of Ignatius Loyola: "to give and not to count the cost." It is the result of God's love that moves our will so that we rise above our natural selfishness. We recognize our kinship with others. By doing so, we act kindly—not grudgingly, but gladly. Our new relation to God causes this action to happen with spontaneity.

In Jesus' story of the Good Samaritan, the man who sincerely loved kindness was the one who helped the beaten traveler lying by the side of the road, not because he had the correct identity card and the right social, racial, and denominational credentials, but because he was a person in distress, a fellow human being who needed the help of other human beings. Loving kindness, like justice, is in the doing of it.

And to walk humbly with your God. The progression Micah sees in the divine demand is one that leads from the doing of justice, to the loving of kindness, to walking, or living, humbly in the presence of God. In that presence we are never alone. We are always with our neighbors. To respond to the appeal of God is to be in his presence where there is fullness of joy evermore.

Now We Know

It is in the obedience of Jesus to his Father that we see what God expects of us in the clearest light. Jesus is the teacher of obedience from whom we learn by obedience. He is the manifestation of God's challenge to and demand upon us. The judgment we have to face, once having seen him, is: *now we know!*

Those who are interested only in ideas or concepts about God will be disappointed to find that Jesus does *not* present us with infallible proofs for God's existence. He shows us what God expects.

At one point of argument with the Pharisees John writes of how Jesus said: "For the Father loves the Son, and shows him all that he himself is doing; and greater works than these will he show him, that you may marvel" (John 5:20). Because of Jesus we know what God wants of us. It is no longer hidden. It is in the light.

In the Gospel of Matthew the basic teachings of Jesus are summed up in the Sermon on the Mount. These teachings are precious. They are also disturbing. They show very clearly that faith and morality cannot be separated. Worship is an everyday experience. It is the personal and moral response to the living God.

It is therefore different from anything expected of us by society. It is diametrically opposed to those demands. According to the myths of our materialistic civilization, riches bring happiness, power brings possessions; to be satiated is to be satisfied, to be praised and flattered is a means of rejoicing.

Now read the Beatitudes and note the difference.

When Thomas More wrote his *Utopia,* he turned to the Sermon on the Mount to show how people should live in love and peace. The commonly accepted values of states were turned upside down. The way of life of Utopia's citizens reflected the revolutionary character of Jesus' teachings. Here, for example, is what they thought of expensive metals: "of gold and silver they commonly make chamber pots." They also loved their enemies. To be in a new relation with God is to show it in our relationships with others.

Because our complete loyalty is to God, our way of living begins in the spirit. In the Sermon on the Mount Jesus stresses that all our actions begin, not with rules, but with obedience in the inward or spiritual life. The character of our intention is revealed in our action. If we love God we shall love our neighbor, not only our neighbor but our enemy. When we love our enemy, by the way, he is no longer our enemy but our neighbor.

To be one with Christ by faith is to know his will and do it. The metaphor of the vine used by Jesus in his final discourses of the Upper Room before his betrayal and execution tells us the source of action. It is in Christ. He is the vine and we are the branches. If we are separated from him, we bear no fruit. We wither and die. The line of creative power is given as follows: "As the Father has loved me, so have I loved you; abide in my love. If you keep my commandments, you will abide in my love (John 15:9–10). "Abiding in love" is surely the key to the fulfilling of God's demand.

The divine love is the silent spring, unseen in its origin, yet bubbling up to be the river of life for all people.

Jesus also made it equally clear that the works of evil are not only in our laws and institutions but in ourselves. Murder is the consequence of hate. Adultery is the fruit of lust. To turn *from* God is to turn to darkness and all that it implies.

Faith In Conflict

The demand of God and the demand of the world cannot be resolved easily. Christian people create their own cultural and moral standards according to their faith. The Christian faith and its expression are continuously in conflict with the prevailing culture of the world.

This should not surprise us. Repeatedly we note that Jesus Christ, his teachings, and his people are different from those societies and institutions that are faithful to political and economic expediency. Frequently, Christians who have opposed certain involvements of their countries, such as the Vietnam conflict or racial segregation, have been told that it is their job to stick to the Gospel and keep out of politics. In support of this view they quote Jesus' answer to the coalition of Pharisees, Sadducees, and Herodians (all, by the way, enemies of each other, united by their hatred of Jesus) when they asked him: "Is it lawful for us to give tribute to Caesar, or not?"

If Jesus had said Yes, the Pharisees would have accused him of blasphemy for not stating that the tribute of God's people should be given to God. If he had stated that tribute should be paid to God alone, then the Herodians would have accused him of plotting the overthrow of Rome. To all intent Jesus was caught on the horns of a dilemma. To affirm Caesar was to be guilty of blasphemy; to affirm God, treason. However, Jesus was not to be caught as easily as that. He asked for a coin. He looked at it, and asked, " 'Whose likeness and inscription has it?' They said, 'Caesar's.' He said to them, 'Then render to Caesar the things that are Caesar's, and to God the things that are God's.' " (Luke 20:24–25).

The roles were reversed. Now the coalition members were on the hot spot. They couldn't answer. Caesar claimed to be divine. Ultimate loyalty to him expressed publicly would have condemned them to the charge of blasphemy. And what remained of their loyalty if they gave it all to God?

Another passage in favor of Christians thinking their faith but not doing it is the one from Romans 13 where Paul tells the Jesus people in Rome to "be subject to the governing authorities." They could hardly be anything else, the power of Rome was so great. If he had said otherwise in his letter, it would have been used against them had it been censored.

To understand the true loyalty to which Paul is referring, it is necessary to read the rest of the chapter. At the eighth verse he writes: "Owe no one anything, except to love one another; for he who loves his neighbor has fulfilled the law. . . . love is the fulfilling of the law."

Jesus never split his loyalty into two parts, one for the nation and one for God. He initiated conflict by demanding all for God. This is the sword he left us to disturb our peace. God comes first. Peter declared this with finality in his address to the Jewish Council in Jerusalem when he stated: "We must obey God rather than men. The God of our fathers raised Jesus whom you killed by hanging him on a tree" (Acts 5:29–30). Those who heard this statement wanted to kill Peter and his fellow apostles, but the intervention of Gamaliel saved their lives.

Many of us today are conscious of the conflict Christ initiated. We have been brought up to be good citizens who uphold the virtues of the West against godless communism. Technocracy, the cult of power, the adoration of success, the worship of affluence, and the supremacy of the state over people are also godless.

There is a conflict of cultures because there are two: one that believes in paying its tribute to Caesar and one that believes in Jesus Christ. We are born into the former. We are reborn into the latter. The most important decision we may make is the one that determines honestly the priority of our loyalties. Remember, we don't have to follow Jesus Christ. We are *free* to follow him. If we do, we have to leave our excuses, our lesser loyalties, our pet prejudices, our tinseled idols behind, and follow him all the way.

What less can he expect of us but all of us: for he gave himself that we might live.

CHAPTER FIVE

What Can You Expect of God?

Your life is changed when you are converted.

I was sitting next to a Swarthmore College student recently and discovered that she was one of the Jesus people. I had thought she was and told her so.

"You can almost always tell, can't you?" she replied smiling.

There *is* something different. It is in their eyes, their whole bearing. In Berkeley I watched one of them trying to raise money for his community, standing on a street corner, shaking a small box with a few coins in it. Love and gentleness were as much a part of his face as were his ears and nose.

Emily Gardiner Neal, who has had extensive experience with spiritual healing, writes in *A Reporter Finds God Through Spiritual Healing:* "There is only one infallible way to receive the power of Jesus Christ: Keep his laws and commandments. Dare to claim his promises, confident that 'God is not a man that he should lie' (Num. 23:19). Realize that 'Without faith it is impossible to please him—he that cometh to God must believe that he is' (Heb. 11:6)."

You will find that God promises four things:

1. Eternal Life

One of the most startling and hard-to-believe promises we have is that of eternal life: "The free gift of God is eternal life in Christ Jesus our Lord" (Rom. 6:23).

No one can possibly conceive of exactly what eternal life is. *The American Heritage Dictionary* gives as a principal definition for "eternal": "Without beginning or end; existing outside of time." The phrase "existing outside of time" is a felicitous one and excites me. In a religious context it has fascinating implications, for time as we know it forms the basic structure of earthly life. God's eternal life is undoubtedly outside of human time. Though the idea is beyond our limited concepts, it is within God's plan for us. Because of this it gives a definite shape and particular meaning to our life.

The specter of death has always troubled mankind. To many people, death means the complete end of life. There is nothing more. But God says that this is not so and through the resurrection of Jesus he has shown this.

2. The Gift of the Holy Spirit

Besides giving us Jesus, the next great gift that God bestowed on the world is the Holy Spirit.

After the crucifixion, Jesus' disciples were a lonely, bewildered group. Their Lord, whom they loved, trusted, and believed to be the Messiah, had been put to death like a common criminal. Then to their ecstatic joy he appeared to them again as he had said he would. He told them to go to Jerusalem and wait, for he promised that God would send his Holy Spirit to be with them and it would be like having Jesus continually in their midst.

An interesting fact is that Jesus gives commands. He does not say: "I think you should do this or that." He says authoritatively: "Do this." If you want to be his follower, if you want to participate fully in all that he has to offer, then you must take his words at face value. He always means exactly what he says, which includes his promise of the Holy Spirit.

His disciples went to Jerusalem. For more than a month they waited, uncertain, questioning, hoping. Yet because Jesus had appeared to them, they believed and obeyed. And they were filled with the Holy Spirit.

The importance of this to you is almost incalculable. Just as the disciples, you too have God's spirit in you. You have within you the spirit of the Creator of the universe!

Various wonderful results flow from this fact.

First, there is what is known as "the fruit of the Spirit." The word "fruit" is singular because one who truly experiences God in Christ within him exhibits all these characteristics. As listed in Galatians 5 they are: love, joy, peace, patience, goodness, kindness, gentleness, faithfulness, and self-control.

These are rare qualities in today's world.

It is no accident that Paul put love and joy first. Jesus' entire emphasis was on love—love of God and love of people. Jesus represents godly traits, and when we know Jesus, we know God and we know God is love.

Certainly one who has the Holy Spirit in him cannot help but be joyous. Many people do not realize the real difference between joy and happiness. The Latin origin of joy is *guadere,* meaning to rejoice. "Happy" apparently comes from the Old Norse *hap,* meaning good luck. The difference is apparent from the beginning.

There is something transitory about happiness. The word almost depends on *things.* A gift might make me happy for a while. Sleeping later in the morning makes some people very happy indeed.

But joy has the feel of something deeper. It is that strong sense of fulfillment or satisfaction that comes from an inner source. Joy is rooted in the depths of our being; the roots of joy are nourished in the deeper earth of love.

The roots of happiness are in shallow ground. In times of hardship when we face the dry winds of adversity, when the soil on the surface of our life becomes hard and dusty, the roots of happiness shrivel and die.

But true joy draws from the living waters of God that run deep through all eternity and never end. This is the deep ground that never dries out, that never changes, that will nourish you always.

And here is the spring that is the fountainhead of joy.

In addition to the "fruit of the Spirit," there are nine manifestations of the Holy Spirit as expressed by Paul in 1 Corinthians 12. These are often overlooked not only by individuals, but unfortunately also by the Church.

These manifestations are: *wisdom* that comes from God's word and the *knowledge* of how to apply it to life; *faith* to produce results to be able to *heal* and perform *miracles* in the name of Jesus Christ; *speaking in tongues* and the *interpretation of tongues;* the ability *to discern between spirits* (between what comes from God or from the devil); and *prophecy,* bringing a message from God that will enlighten or comfort people.

Anyone who has been converted can manifest these gifts. At the direction of the Holy Spirit, to fill a particular need at a given time, we will be more active in some than in others. But as heirs of God this gift is within you to express. We do not need any special training, for example, to be an instrument of God's healing touch. You were given the means to do this when you received the Holy Spirit. These manifestations are to be used to help others as well as to enlighten yourself.

3. Order Out of Chaos

Contrary to what some believe, our universe is *not* chaotic. Think of the seasons, how they move with regularity, "the stars in their course." The reason that scientists can send our astronauts into outer space is that they can count on the predictability of certain forces.

It is true we live in a world of multiple choices, and because of this, unless you have a basis to judge what will or will not fit into your life, your existence will be chaotic. But this is your fault. If you have no criterion by which to base your selections, when unexpected events occur you will be uncertain as to what is the best decision.

Most mental illness is based either on the internal conflict between opposing ideas—the individual cannot determine which to accept or reject—or on the fear of separation, of being rejected. We could say that Satan, having been forced from God's presence because of his rebellion, brought his anxieties and fears to earth.

A simple illustration is someone ordering from a large menu in a restaurant. He makes choices knowing what he can afford, likes, and what will agree with him. His choices are the result of his disciplined freedom.

When Christ becomes the center of your life, you begin to live a more orderly existence. You are able to choose and reject far more easily because you know what will fit into your life. Life begins to take on more purpose because it has definite shape to it. The inner conflict is resolved.

In a sense all existence *is* relative. But you must ask always; relative to what? If your life is relative to a false premise, your error will become obvious though you may never understand what went wrong or how to change circumstances.

A life relative to Christ brings light to you and to the world, for God is the center. As an heir your life is simpler, neater, more joyous, and purposeful. There is an explosive kind of joy to being a Christian that makes you want to share it. "In him was life, and the life was the light of men" (John 1:4).

4. The Freedom To Become Yourself

Paul Tournier, a leading psychiatrist and devout Christian, suggests that

God wills the development of all men. When from time to time he makes them hear his call to self-denial, to renunciation, and even self-sacrifice, it is not for their impoverishment, but for their enrichment. Christianity is in full accord with psychology. Like psychology, it sees man in continual evolution from a lesser condition to a greater one, from limited freedom to greater freedom, from poor wealth to truer wealth. The Gospel of Jesus Christ is nothing if not a gospel of growth. It sets our eyes on a development more complete than any that can be conceived by a psychology confined within the limits of nature.*

What a gloriously optimistic statement. So often people are turned away from Christianity because of a misconception. They believe erroneously that it represents a negative, limiting approach to life. But this is not true. Christianity is built on hope, on optimism, on great expectations. It is the rest of the world that is negative and lives in fear—fear of poverty, fear of sickness, fear of death, fear of what people think.

"From a lesser condition to a greater one." It is not only addicts

A Place for You (New York: Harper & Row, 1966).

of every sort—alcohol, drug, sex—that go on to a greater condition. The words apply to everyone.

You grow in understanding your life's purpose, in relating your own life to all of life. You grow in strength to do what you know must be done and you are given the power to cope with all situations. You grow to a greater freedom, for you are no longer a prisoner of yourself.

This is what is meant by the passage from Galatians 4:7. You are no longer a "slave" to habits, social pressures, fear. You are not at the mercy of cycles and events. You are not predestined by the stars. You are becoming truly free, for you are becoming yourself, what God intended you to be.

In *The Strange Life of Ivan Osokin,* the magician explains to Ivan that: "I said that you cannot change anything and that nothing will change by itself. I have already told you, that in order to change anything you must first change yourself. And this is much more difficult than you think."

Ivan was a prisoner of himself, repeating the same stupid mistakes. We are all Ivans until released by God.

When Tournier speaks of going from poorer to truer wealth, he means that we become less enamored by things, by status and position in the world. We develop an understanding of what makes up the really permanent values of life, "where neither moth nor rust consumes and where thieves do not break in and steal" (Matt. 6:20). It is not that material things are bad in themselves. They simply have to be seen in the proper perspective. They are not the goal in life. They are meant to be used *for* life.

The Prisoner of Second Avenue is a comedy by Neil Simon about a modern couple living in New York who are trapped by circumstances into remaining there. At one point—out of a job, out of money, out of morale—the protagonist picks up a musical jigger that fits on top of liquor bottles and swears at it angrily. He is appalled that such a silly gadget could have once meant so much to him. He cursed the money wasted on things like that. And what did he have to show for it? "Nothing but a god-damned gimmick!"

And so we become free of being shackled to things. No longer are they the foundation of our happiness, the criteria of our success.

Perhaps the most succinct summary of the Christian life as far as what God expects of us and what we in turn may expect of him is contained in Luke 6:36–38: "Be merciful, even as your Father is merciful. Judge not, and you will not be judged; condemn not, and you will not be condemned; forgive and you will be forgiven; give and it will be given to you; good measure, pressed down, shaken together, running over, will be put into your lap."

That is God's promise.

CHAPTER SIX

Love, Marriage, and Sex

Love!

Has anything been more overwritten about, less understood and experienced, more greatly desired and needed, more heroically practiced, more talked about than love? It is a perennial favorite of philosophers, social commentators, ministers, priests, rabbis, college students, and concerned citizens.

It is so much in our minds, because though it is the essence of life's meaning, there is so little of it around. Love embodies all that is best in life; knowing that we search for it.

To give love and to be loved completes the magic circle of fulfillment. When you give love you are giving yourself to the one, to the others. When you receive love you are receiving the *other* into you.

One of the most glorious poems is the one by Paul on love, 1 Corinthians 13. The words sing, the thoughts surround us like life itself. They speak not only to our hearts, but also to our minds and souls.

What is this love that is patient and kind, neither arrogant nor rude, neither emphemeral nor fickle, lasting as long as time itself?

Love is like life. It must exist to be known.

The Revolution of Love

For Paul, love is the fulfillment of faith. Faith is the potential, the possibility. But love is the catalyst that activates it.

There is nothing on earth more important than love. Nothing! Without love we become inhuman. To the extent that we love, we grow toward whatever is best in human life. Any human relationship without love is abnormal.

It will be through love that ultimately the world's tragic problems will be resolved. The brilliance of scientists and the leadership of politicians will be directed toward a common end. The politics of love will be the principal ethic. There can be only one kind of successful revolution: *a revolution of love.* This is the revolution that Jesus initiated and in which we continue.

The problem is that most people yearn *to be loved.*

What they should yearn for is *to love.*

And within those few words lies the difference between happiness and unhappiness, fulfillment and separation, peace and war.

The Three Kinds of Love

Because human beings are complicated, so is love.

English, that incomparably rich language with over 600,000 words and more synonyms per word than any other language, has only one word to cover all the aspects and subtleties of love. The unabridged *Webster's Third New International Dictionary* lists sixteen major catagories of meaning for love.

How casually we use the word. "I *love* my work." "Don't you *love* that dress?" "I'm in *love.*" "*Love* one another as I have *loved* you." In tennis you can win a *love* game.

Other languages do better, and the Greeks seem to have been the most articulate. They have three words that designate broadly the principal areas of love.

Eros (*er*-os) is associated with desire; the state of being in love when we first fall in love; of seeking self-fulfillment; of being pleasure-directed. It is most commonly associated with sexuality.

Philia (fil-*e*-a) is brotherly love. It is affection and friendship. It is a sense of slippers, a sweater and slacks, and an evening spent with old friends. It is a courteous answer to a question, the pleasure of a casual acquaintance.

Agape (ag-*a*-pay) is the most complicated and important love, for it is the love shown by God in his action of forgiveness and redemption of mankind through Jesus Christ. It is sacrificial love, given freely for the sake of the other; it does not look for a reward or response. It is the type of love Jesus speaks of: "This is my commandment, that you love one another as I have loved you. Greater love has no man than this, that a man lay down his life for his friends. You are my friends if you do what I command you" (John 15:12–14). This is a love that must be acquired, and the very young do not come by it naturally. It is the kind of love we should aspire to as we grow in our understanding of faith. Faith and agape are closely related.

These three loves intermingle in our lives, but the one least often found and the most needed is agape. On it hangs the fate of our world.

Roots of Love

When Jesus was asked which was the greatest commandment, he replied that the first was to love God. Then he continued: "And a second is like it, You shall love your neighbor as yourself " (Matt. 22:37–39).

The New Testament makes two important points about love.

First, Paul considers love, as exemplified by the Gospel, as the fulfillment of faith in action. You know that through your conversion Christ lives in you. But you know also that it is by your loving actions in the world that you live in Christ. You are, in this way, more truly a follower of his, for your faith is being expressed in active love for your "neighbor."

"For in Christ Jesus neither circumcision nor uncircumcision is of any avail, but faith working through *love*. . . . For you were called to freedom, brethren; only do not use your freedom as an opportunity for the flesh, but through *love* be servants of one another. For the whole law is fulfilled in one word, 'You shall love your neighbor as yourself' " (Gal. 5:6, 13–14).

The new Christian should be warned that as he reads the Sermon on the Mount and the many parables and sayings that Jesus used to illustrate love he may be tempted to say: "Now I know exactly what God expects of me." This is a trap similar to the one the Pharisees built for themselves. They had everything worked out as to what constituted the holy life. They interpreted the Scripture legalistically rather than observing the underlying spirit.

The Sermon on the Mount and the other examples are paradigms of love. They are indicatives rather than imperatives. In them Jesus leads us to an appreciation of the magnitude of love, showing us in full the spirit of love in action.

Another fact is that you will never really know ahead of time just what God expects of you in a particular situation until that moment arrives. All you know is that there is only one commandment in the New Testament: to love. And at the right time God will show you the type of loving action that is demanded of you, if you have ears to hear, eyes to see, and a heart to believe and to love.

What will be demanded of you rarely will be heroic, though there may be a few times in your life when God's call to love will seem to be beyond your capacity. But as you go out in faith he will supply whatever you need.

The phrase "love your neighbor as yourself" is quoted continually as an ethic of conduct by as many non-Christians as Christians. But the whole point of the thought is missed if it is quoted apart from the first portion: "You shall love the Lord your God with all your heart, and with all your soul, and with all your mind. This is the great and first commandment" (Matt. 22:37–38, Deut. 6:5). "And a second is like it . . ."

If we love a "neighbor" within the context of the entire statement we will be loving as Jesus wishes, for as we love God so will the same kind of love spill over to our "neighbor." And loving our "neighbor" is the only real and tangible way we can show our love for God. If we just follow the injunction "to love your neighbor as yourself" we are on thin ground for loving. We have already too much self-love in us as it is. How will we be able to love others when we are so much in love with ourselves? No, we need God to help us love our "neighbor."

Further, my estimate of myself may not be accurate. I may either underrate or overvaluate myself. I know a man who had this to say about the Golden Rule, which is another way of stating the second commandment: "Do unto others as I would have them do unto me? Well, I don't expect people to help me, and I don't expect to help them."

Such a love as this, whatever there is of it, will be based on "feeling," and "feeling" is a flimsy scaffold on which to build a permanent ethic.

The second important point to realize about the New Testament and love is that the meaning of love, as exemplified in the life of Jesus Christ, becomes the guideline for all human relations. His life becomes the basis for an ethic of love. This kind of love has the power to transform our small earthly loves of philia and eros from limited selfish loving to what is really the apex of one's loving nature: the gift of ourselves to someone else's need, *even when we do not like that person.*

That is love. That is agape. Love such as this is always doing extraordinary things.

How difficult it is to achieve this kind of love. How often I stumble about clumsily in this area. My daily prayer for years is that God will teach me to love better. I need this. As most of us, I fall short of what is expected. But this is the human condition. Our hope and God's promise is that with our sincere efforts and his help we will grow.

Love Misunderstood

Once I edited a small magazine. We were young, enthusiastic, and idealistic. Our budget was tiny. Despite the fact that we could only afford to pay authors a small amount of money, many famous people wrote for us since there was no other publication where they could air their deepest feelings about human and spiritual values.

I contacted a well-known anthropologist-sociologist about doing an article. He had written extensively about ethics and he was just the right person to do what I had in mind. He accepted with enthusiasm and I was thrilled.

Some months later, to my dismay and utter astonishment, I came across the article in one of the mass media publications—the exact title, subject matter—everything just as I had outlined them to him.

When I telephoned him he apologized and then excused himself on the basis that the magazine paid far more than we did.

I was so shocked and shattered I could only hang up. Here was a man known throughout the world as a writer on ethics and love and this was his response!

My wife, normally somewhat shy, was so incensed she telephoned him back immediately and said she was ashamed that someone of his stature could so betray a trust.

His first response was that after all this was a business deal and one treats one's friends and family one way and others in another.

She then proceeded to give him one of the finest talks on ethics I have ever heard. In the end he had nothing to say at all. Though famous, he was a very embarrassed man.

His concept of love was typical of many people. It was a most limited form of philia. It had no depth, no awareness of the real meaning of love. As Jesus tells us, it is easy to love those who love you. Even nonbelievers do that (Matt. 5:43–47).

A fashion magazine quoted a young, beautiful, popular actress:

I need always to keep a sense of myself as an independent person, to continue to search for the authentic in me, the natural. Love is the best thing in the world, but in a relationship, the important thing is not to lose oneself, not to become someone else. You must be complete before you can love or be loved —the only person who can help you is you.

Her approach typifies a current mood. It is the antithesis of Christian love, for where Christian love is warm and concerned, hers is cool, uninvolved, self-contained, reluctant to give of herself. In its own way her reaction mirrors what psychiatrist Erich Fromm describes as the sickness of our age: the feeling of separation between people. It might be something of a non sequitur, but I could not help noticing that out of eight photographs there is not one smile on this beautiful face.

She does not understand that you only begin to find yourself in other people. You cannot fully know yourself by lonely introspection, or by not commiting yourself to the world. Yes, when you love fully, you make yourself vulnerable to pain and heartbreak. But you open yourself to greater love and joy as well.

This actress will always be seeking but never finding. Until she gives of herself fully in the sense of philia and agape she cannot begin to love as she wants to. Her love at the moment is eros, desire.

She represents an attitude among many young people that sexual relationships outside of marriage are not only acceptable, but to be expected.

This is a sensitive area in our society, for its ramifications extend far beyond what is thought to be a casual, personal act. What is involved are important underlying values that influence an entire approach to life.

Many young people simply are not aware of this. They have no concept of the long-term harmful influence casual sex will have on their lives.

The Bible's attitude is that sexuality is a normal function of life. It is not critical of the sex urge itself, but only of greedy desire.

But because of the temptation to immorality, each man should have his own wife and each woman her own husband. The husband should give to his wife her conjugal rights, and likewise the wife to her husband. For the wife does not rule over her own body, but the husband does; likewise the husband does not rule over his own body, but the wife does. Do not refuse one another except perhaps by agreement for a season, that you may devote yourselves to prayer; but then come together again, lest Satan tempt you through lack of self-control (1 Cor. 7:2–5).

The Human Sex Act Is Not an Isolated Function

Sexuality is a dimension of personal existence in which the meaning of love is to be learned and in which love between persons reaches a depth, intimacy and creativity of expression which is incomparable with most other loves. Love at this depth means the giving of faithful devotion to another person on terms which do not threaten or corrupt that devotion. Christianity in its essence does not look upon sex as something which belongs to the lowest part of human nature, but as a power which leads to one of the highest forms of communion.*

The problems of sex must be studied through a wide-angle lens encompassing the whole range of love. The love between a man and a woman has the possibility of representing all love: eros, philia,

*Daniel Day Williams, *The Spirit and the Forms of Love* (New York: Harper & Row, 1968).

agape. Within such a relationship a couple is a microcosm, a world in miniature of what can be the most beautiful in love, or it can represent what is most ugly and sordid.

A major difficulty confusing the issue is that many people tend to isolate the sexual act. They treat it as an activity that is somehow independent from the whole of one's life. This is impossible to do. The mind and the body are as one. Each gland, each organ is interrelated. Whatever we do that involves one part of ourself, physical or mental, involves the whole.

An added complication is that sex is one of the most vital, powerful forces in our lives. When it is combined with full love, it is a source of joy and beauty that spills over and permeates all other portions of our life. When it is misunderstood and not kept in perspective, one's life becomes like a camera out of focus. The picture it takes is faulty, the scene misrepresented. It is out of balance.

"The evil in the life of sex is the isolated function, which manifests its hostility to the divine order by reducing the awe inspiring process of procreating and sexual union to a mere trifle."*

Commitment Sustains Love

Today we live in a society that is inundated by sex symbols. Magazines, books, films, popular spokesmen from the arts, articulate pornography—all pressure for a promiscuous society, for a society with few or no restraints on sex.

It is surprising that despite these pressures so many people have retained a sensible attitude. Marriage and commitment are still the balance wheel of civilization.

It will be easiest if we look at love and sex within the framework of marriage, for it is a relationship between two people that can be constructive or destructive. It mirrors the world. Because all three kinds of love are involved, it also illustrates how people come to be mature. We learn to love in our associations with others.

There must be first an initial strong physical attraction between the two people. They are "in love" and their feelings run high. At this

*Emil Brunner, *The Divine Imperative* (Philadelphia: Westminster Press, 1947).

point their love is mostly eros, desire and yearning. It is a love that says, "I love you because you are attractive to me." "I love myself and want you to love me too."

It is a "feeling" love. One of the most predictable qualities about eros or "feeling" love is its unpredictability. Feeling is not dependable because it is always changing. It is an emotion that is not anchored to anything substantial. It so easily breaks loose from its moorings at the slightest wind of adversity.

A relationship that depends on feeling cannot last, for eros feelings come and go. Eros love in a marriage is important, of course, and should be present if there is going to be full happiness, but it is only a part of a whole. Our love can grow only if it is based on qualities that encourage love.

A flower cannot grow if the soil is not properly nourished. Love will not grow if the soil of the relationship is acid and barren.

The essential ingredient that is necessary is commitment. Perhaps another way of expressing it is fidelity, a word that embodies so much that is important to our whole approach to life, even beyond marriage. It involves the unfailing fulfillment of one's duties and obligations and the keeping of one's word or vows. It expresses loyalty. It implies an inner responsibility that helps you to stand up to your obligations.

It is true, of course, that marriage springs from love, but its stability is based not on love alone, but on fidelity. Fidelity is the ethical element which enhances natural love, and only by its means does the natural become personal. It is, therefore, the only quality which can guarantee the permanence of the marriage relation. Through the marriage vows the feeling of love is absorbed into the personal will; this alone provides the guarantee to the other party which justifies the venture of such a life companionship. Marriage which is based only upon love (eros and/or philia) is inevitably accompanied by the fear that love may fade, and thus the dissolution of the marriage.*

The young who are concerned that marriage inevitably sinks into dull duty should know the glorious fact that commitment and fidelity nourish the love in a marriage; consequently love is always being renewed and made fresh and clean and exciting.

The full love we are discussing is not words. Love is deeds. Big

---

*Brunner, *The Divine Imperative.*

deeds and little deeds. It is doing things for the other person when we really do not "feel" like it. It is easy to do something when it does not bother us or when we "feel" happy. It is more difficult when we do not "feel" this way.

Such a love now begins to combine all three loves. The relationship between a man and a woman is complete. The fullness of the sexual experience is realized as at no other time. Because it is a physical *and* spiritual union it embodies all of life: life's pleasures, life's mysteries, life's sense of completion and fulfillment. It is a holy trinity of God, man, and woman. There is no longer separation.

Perhaps sexual love within the Judeo-Christian framework is the most satisfactory because

If the chief end of man is to glorify God and enjoy him forever, this includes the sexual life. One of the symptoms of sickness in the treatment of sexuality in much modern literature is that there is too little gratitude for it. Sex is treated as a torment, or possession, or weapon against the world; but the note of gratitude for sexuality as enrichment of life, for ecstatic joy and the serenity of faithful companionship, all this gets left out of the meaning of sex.*

Though the emphasis here is on marriage, there are many individuals who are able to live happy, successful lives who are not married. By creatively redirecting their sexual drives into other areas of life, they too have a similar potential to grow to a fullness of love and understanding.

Love is the essence of life. It is the joy, the cement, the salt, the strength, the spark, and the light. The New Testament raises love above all else.

Those outside the Judeo-Christian faiths can love, of course, deeply and sensitively. But from the experience of such love a whole dimension will be lacking. It will be difficult for them to grasp the essence of agape.

Promiscuity Warps and Stunts Love

The problems of the world are due to an absence of love, to a misunderstanding of love. This is no simplistic assessment, but a basic, tragic truth.

*Williams, *The Spirit and the Forms of Love.*

Young people sense the reality of this observation and it is one reason why they are so concerned about the hypocrisy they find running throughout public and private lives like a disease. There is not much peace in the world and the loss of ideals haunts them. They search for integrity, commitment, and a spirit of agape love.

Many do not realize, however, that the spirit of *full* love is warped and stunted through sexual promiscuity, and so they deny themselves the very thing they long for.

In a subtle, insidious way that is difficult to comprehend at first, sex outside the bonds of marriage tends to limit one's capacity to love. In a sexual relationship outside of marriage, we will be exploiting our "neighbor" for selfish reasons even though our actions may be hidden under the most eloquent words. The arguments for such casual sex are specious, for there is no commitment to the other person, no real fidelity. Love is misunderstood. These arguments may make it all seem reasonable and desirable, but it is based on a false premise.

The young too often approach one of the major steps in their lives as if in a romantic dream. The hard realities have been blurred under a barrage of propaganda. They do not see that life can be hard and terribly cruel to the unwary, to the naïve and foolishly impetuous.

Furthermore, those who have lived sexually with others later seem to have more difficulty finding a marriage partner whom they really love and trust, and who in return will fully love, trust, and care for them. Because this element of trust is lost, the marriage is weakened even before it begins.

A happy marriage has to be based on trust in one's spouse, for trust is the dynamic that enables a couple to live together freely, not as prisoners of suspicion and jealousy.

Publicity surrounding attractive men and women in the arts makes casual sex seem glamorous. But the outsider does not realize what empty souls these people have and how little they actually contribute to life. Their own lives are usually a tangled mass of frustration and disappointment. As they grow older they wonder why joy and mature loving relationships have eluded them.

George Sanders, the sophisticated, charming actor, ended his life by suicide. His final philosophy was: "I'm a cynic. Our values are all false and life is simply a matter of pretense. The whole world is a sham. It's just boring. I don't know where society is going and I don't care—I'm just happy I won't be around to see it. I have no friends, no interests, no plans."

Future Hope

Until today restraint has come from outside pressures. In the past public opinion, legalities, the Church's disapproval, and fear of pregnancy have hindered promiscuity. In other words, our sexual values have come from factors outside of ourselves rather than from within. Now that these restraints no longer exist there is less and less protection from outside for precious human relationships against corruption and degradation.

This could be a dramatically hopeful sign, for it means that now at last our values must be developed from within us. In the past obedience has been through fear rather than love. Now it must come from love. There is a vast difference between the two approaches and it could lead mankind into an entirely new way of perceiving life.

The real problem is that most of us are unaware and selfish. We tend to do what pleases us at the moment. We do not consider how our actions may affect the whole fabric of society.

Fads come and go. One of the fads that reappears in history is that of sexual permissiveness. It may be new to our particular age, but it is not historically new. People clamor loudly in print and on television about the new morals. But they are not new. It's all happened before. It's the same person dressed in a different suit of clothes. The cities of Sodom and Gomorrah (Genesis 19) 2000 years before Christ, for example, illustrate sexual depravity. What is it that goads mankind into forgetting history so that he must relearn again and again its painful lessons?

There are new elements in our age: atomic energy, the frightening advances in biology where life may be manufactured and controlled. These are new. But sexual permissiveness is not. What would be new is a society that truly understands the concept of love. And then violence, unhappiness and despair would be far less frequent. The trouble is that most people won't take the time to understand love. Perhaps they fear that love's demands may be too much for them.

The paradox is that loving commitment generates love.

What we should do in order to make a new beginning is to take to heart these words of Paul in his second letter to Timothy: "God did not give us a spirit of timidity but a spirit of power and love and self-control" (2 Tim. 1:7).

CHAPTER SEVEN

Divine Healing

C. S. Lewis writes in *Miracles*: "All the essentials of Hinduism would, I think, remain unimpaired if you subtracted the miraculous, and the same is almost true of Islam. But you cannot do that with Christianity. It is precisely the story of a great Miracle. A naturalistic Christianity leaves out all that is specifically Christian."

Christianity is the only religion that has a ministry of healing based on a supreme miracle. Christianity depends completely on the resurrection of Jesus Christ. No other religion has dared to rest its appeal on a miracle, and out of that one miracle to promise the possibility of salvation for the whole human race.

The ancient words used at the end of Christian healing services since the first century have brought comfort and hope to millions: "Go, believing that thou art healed."

The telephone rang late at night.

Anne was calling to say that David, her husband, was critically ill from another heart attack and was expected to die at any moment. He had been in the hospital for two weeks.

David was fifty-four years old. He had retired from business partly because of his heart condition. His oldest daughter was married and he had a son in the middle teens. He was a gentle, serious man and, though not a native of this country, his sincere interest in people and in his community made him many friends. I could not believe it was his time to die.

Though he lived over 300 miles away my wife and I decided that we would go to him and pray for his healing.

Anne thoroughly expected her husband to die. In fact she said it would be a blessing, he was so uncomfortable. The doctor stated categorically that there was no hope for him at all and that it was only a matter of a few days or a week at the most before he would surely die. Only a small part of his heart was still functioning properly.

When we walked into his hospital room he did not seem to recognize us at first. His voice was so weak and blurred we could not understand him.

I explained that we were going to pray that his physical health be improved, for we have God's promise that when two or three are gathered together in Jesus' name that our prayers will be answered. Though David belonged to a church and was as active as his health allowed, he knew nothing about Divine Healing.

Placing my hand over his heart, we prayed that God would remove his pain and sickness and restore him to health in the name of Jesus Christ.

About ten minutes later his evening meal was brought in. For the past two weeks he had been unable to feed himself, eating virtually nothing. Now, to Anne's astonishment, he sat up, his legs dangling over the side of the bed, and fed himself. His voice was much stronger and color was coming back into his face. Three weeks later he took a 2000-mile plane trip to spend several months in a warmer climate with a brother. Later that year he journeyed the 300 miles from his home to be with us during Thanksgiving Day.

David died two years later. But it had been a period of grace, for he had seen a new grandchild and helped his wife establish herself in a business in which she was proficient. He indicated to his family that now he was ready to go.

Shortly before my co-author was to leave Scotland for America, he made a parish visit to a woman who had terminal cancer of her internal organs. The doctor had given her no more than six months to live; the six months had passed.

"Do you believe in faith healing?" she asked Mr. Gordon.

"I believe in the healing power of God."

"Would you pray for me?"

Of course he would. "Do you believe that Jesus Christ is Lord?"

"I do."

"Are you willing to put your life in God's hands for his will to be done?"

She was.

He laid his hand on her and said a prayer for healing.

A week later she was out of bed. The edema was gone, and she felt stronger. Soon after she went to see the surgeon, who acknowledged that the cancer had recessed.

She lived another seven years and her family said that she had had a complete personality change. Previously she had been "house proud," more concerned about her home and furnishings than her family. The were amazed at how sweet she had become as a wife and mother.

For a year I had been feeling extremely ill. An ulcer was suspected. One morning I awakened early and for some reason pressed around my abdomen and discovered a large lump. Having been a medicine editor at one time, the other symptoms together with an extremely low blood count made me suspect it was a tumor, probably malignant. I felt confident that with God's help all would turn out well. In fact I was so confident I went back to sleep. Within five days I was in the operating room.

The night before my operation I asked our minister to say a healing prayer for me. Though he was a man of deep faith he felt inadequate. Erroneously he believed he should have some kind of special training. Nonetheless he prayed, and so did others. The surgeon himself was a religious man.

When I was wheeled into the operating room I truly felt I was on the wings of prayer. I had no fear. I *knew* everything would be all right. I cannot tell you how I knew. It was just an absolute certitude.

After the operation the surgeon, who did not know of my own faith, said that he had never had an operation go as well. "It was like a miracle." The malignant tumor was large and the disease advanced.

That occurred years ago. It was an intense spiritual experience for me and I would not have given up one moment of it. In many ways this was a turning point in my faith, when I became aware of God's presence as never before.

The young man was a superb athlete. Though he had mononucleosis and hepatitis he finished the football season, for as the local star he didn't want to let his community down.

Later, when the team won the regional championship, the town sent the boys to Washington, D.C., as a treat. The weather was bad and unfortunately they drank heavily.

The young man become desperately ill and was rushed home. An operation was necessary. The found that certain critical ducts were blocked and he would undoubtedly die within the week. In fact his aunt, a surgeon who assisted at the operation, confirmed this prognosis. She said the situation was hopeless.

His mother was on the verge of a breakdown.

Ernest Gordon was present and felt that they ought not give up all hope. " 'It may not be God's will for him to die at this time,' I told them. I wanted them to think about that. Later I planned to come back and have a communion service with them and the boy.

"After communion I put my hand on the boy's head. As I prayed I was conscious of a release of power.

"Within a few days the boy's condition changed dramatically. He went back to the hospital for a checkup and his blood count was normal. The surgeon did not believe this was possible. The boy called back the following week and eventually was pronounced clear."

Skeptics will say that these illustrations either were spontaneous remissions or simply a matter of luck. But these are only a few examples out of many that each of the authors of this book has experienced directly. Furthermore, through our acquaintance with people engaged in Divine Healing, or those reputable authors reporting about the subject, we know of innumerable cases similar to those we have presented. Every day throughout the world "miracles" are taking place.

Many such healings are instantaneous.

In *A Reporter Finds God Through Spiritual Healing*, Emily Gardiner Neal tells about her first exposure to a Divine Healing service.* A large goiter on the neck of a woman vanished and the hands of a young boy that were completely covered with warts were instantly

*New York: Morehouse-Barlow Co., 1956.

made clear, his skin healthy and smooth.

At evangelist Kathryn Kuhlman's healing services in Los Angeles and Pittsburgh, literally unbelievable "miracles" take place time after time. People confined to wheelchairs or bed for an endless array of reasons get up and walk; a pair of eyes incurably blinded years before by an accident with molten steel see again; a veteran dying of earlier wounds attends a service as a last hope and is immediately healed; terminal cancer patients ready to die within days walk out well.

These cases are not hearsay. They are well documented and attested to by the doctors who have treated the people.

When you see such things with your own eyes you become aware of not only the power of God, but also of his love and mercy.

Is Divine Healing new? Is it something esoteric, strange, and foreign? Do people have to have some special gift either to be a channel for healing others or to be healed?

The answer is no.

Too often the Church forgets that Jesus spent much of his ministry healing the sick. You may recall the incident in Matthew 11 when John the Baptist, in prison, sent word to Jesus: " 'Are you he who is to come, or shall we look for another?' And Jesus answered them, 'Go and tell John what you hear and see: the blind receive their sight and the lame walk, lepers are cleansed and the deaf hear, and the dead are raised up, and the poor have good news preached to them' " (11:3–5).

What is significant about Jesus' healing was that it was a dramatic way of introducing people to the Gospel of the Good News he preached. It was a visible sign of God's power and mercy for everyone to see. And it was evidence that the rule of God was present.

There are a number of healings in the Old Testament, and the New Testament abounds in examples as well as giving exhortations to heal. "Heal the sick, raise the dead, cleanse lepers, cast out demons" (Matt. 10:8). "And many followed him, and he healed them all" (Matt. 12:15). "Is any one among you suffering? Let him pray. Is any cheerful? Let him sing praise. Is any among you sick? Let him call for the elders of the church, and let them pray over him, anointing him with oil in the name of the Lord; and the prayer of faith will save the sick man, and the Lord will raise him up; and if he has committed sins, he will be forgiven" (James 5:13–15).

A basic difference exists between "faith" healing and Divine or

Spiritual Healing. We can have faith in an object such as a talisman or a doctor. It may buoy our spirits. In the event of hysteria or psychological illness, such a faith may even effect a cure. Witchcraft presumes to conjure up either good or bad spirits. But let there be no mistake in the reality of Jesus the Christ. Within him lies the *heart* of the universe. His is the ultimate power. True healing comes only from God.

Christian Science is known for its emphasis on healing. Though it relies on the Bible, the principal difference in approach is that the Christian Scientists regard man as essentially spiritual and therefore incapable of evil. They believe that man's regeneration comes from an understanding of God and of keeping in mind a perfect image of himself. They do not believe it is necessary to use doctors.

Many of our ministers and laymen overlook the fact that in the early years of the Church there was nothing strange about Divine Healing. It was an accepted part of Christian life. If one was not healed either he or those ministering to him were suspected of unconfessed sin. The early Church Fathers such as Irenaeus, Tertullian, and Origen were authentic witnesses to Divine Healing. "In the name of Jesus Christ, our Christian men have healed and do heal," stated Justin Martyr in the second century.

In our time there seems to be a return to this important part of the Church ministry. Because there is some misunderstanding about the phenomenon, it will be helpful to see the prevailing conditions under which healings most often take place.

1. Faith and Expectation

Faith is the sine qua non of the religious experience. It is essential both for the one being healed and the healer. Jesus replies consistently to those who beseech him: "According to your faith."

Kathryn Kuhlman says that "faith is more than belief; it is more than confidence; it is more than trust, and above all it is never boastful. If your faith is powerless, it is not faith. You cannot have faith without results anymore than you can have motion without movement. The thing we sometimes call faith is only trust. But although we trust in the Lord, it is *faith* which has action and power."

J. Cameron Peddie, a Scottish minister and a pioneer in the modern healing movement, writes: "I will say that for me the highest type of degree of faith is a vivid sense of co-operation with God."

He goes on to say:

Many humble and good folk feel that they have not enough faith to receive benefit from the ministry, but I cannot write too emphatically that they need have no such fear. While faith at its highest and best is essential in the one who ministers, and while patients who have great and simple faith are more responsive and easier to heal, those who have no faith in God, or in this form of ministry, can most surprisingly be healed. It seems as if in his infinite compassion, he cannot resist their need.*

Again and again I find that those who have been healed came with the *expectancy* that they would be healed. They took Jesus' words at face value. C.S. Lewis called his autobiography *Surprised by Joy.* Sometimes people are unexpectedly "surprised by faith." When you take one step toward Christ, he takes two toward you. Love is something you do. It is faith in action.

2. Focusing Attention on Jesus and the Holy Spirit

Too much of the time we focus our attention on ourselves, our problems and our goals. We are concerned about money, and whether our plans will materialize. We think that when we solve these normal worries, we will have the peace and time to think about religion. Jesus, however, tells us that we have things backward.

So do not start worrying: "Where will my food come from, or my drink, or my clothes?" (These are the things the heathen are always after.) Your Father in heaven knows that you need all these other things. So do not worry about tomorrow; it will have enough worries of its own. There is no need to add to the troubles each day brings (Matt. 6:31–34, *Good News for Modern Man*).

This is no promise of wealth or fame. It simply states the fact that if you put yourself in God's hands you should no longer fret, for he

**The Forgotten Talent* (London: Fontana Books, 1966).

knows your particular needs better than you do. Your life will be fuller and happier than you can imagine. Look to Christ. Be a follower of his. Try to grow in a spiritual sense.

A young lawyer was discussing healing with me and wondered if it were not possible that healing was some latent power of the mind that during the evolution of time might become available to everyone. Mankind *is* gradually developing and much will happen that now seems implausible. But it does no good to try to second guess God. We should relax in Jesus' promise that the healing power of the Holy Spirit is available to us—*now*!

3. The Power of the Name Jesus Christ

Now Peter and John were going up to the temple at the hour of prayer, the ninth hour. And a man lame from birth was being carried, whom they laid daily at that gate of the temple which is called Beautiful to ask alms of those who entered the temple. Seeing Peter and John about to go into the temple, he asked for alms. And Peter directed his gaze at him, with John, and said, "Look at us." And he fixed his attention upon them, expecting to receive something from them. But Peter said, 'I have no silver and gold, but I give you what I have; *in the name of Jesus Christ of Nazareth,* walk (Acts 3:1–6).

This authority to heal in Jesus' name came from him: "Truly, truly, I say to you, he who believes in me will also do the works that I do; and greater works than these will he do, because I go to the Father. Whatever you ask in my name, I will do it, that the Father may be glorified in the Son; if you ask anything in my name, I will do it" (John 14:12–14).

It was known in the early Church that the name of Jesus held a particular power. Emily Gardiner Neal has suggested that this may in time be confirmed scientifically by means of radiaethesia, a branch of science based on the measurement of wave lengths coming from the body. She reports that the name of Jesus and the sign of the cross affect to a very real degree radiation coming from the body.

Some of the physical effects that people notice in healing are those of heat, pressure, and pain. Frequently you hear descriptions: "like an electric shock," "intense heat," "a burning sensation," "it was as though my insides were being scalded." When you are close by it seems sometimes as if the individual has a fever.

During a healing service at Trinity Cathedral in Trenton, New Jersey, I was aware of heat emanating from a body while I knelt at the altar praying for someone desperately ill. At first I thought it was the person next to me, but then realized it came from Dean Lloyd Chattin who was ministering to someone two or three people away. As he approached it grew in intensity. Later, when I asked him if he were aware of this phenomenon, he said he was not.

4. Fasting

Though fasting is not necessarily a prerequisite for healing, frequently people fast who are either praying for others or who themselves are asking for healing. It seems to be a natural, spiritual step to take.

Historically, fasting is part of a total approach to a deeper spiritual experience. In its own way "it is an expression of the fervor of our prayers." It is an act of love and of faith. The small discomfort and the breaking of the three-time daily habit of eating for a short while is a modest offering to God for all that he has given.

During your fast you are aware of a greater sense of peace. In religious terms, it leads to a "quickening of the spirit." It is as though you were preparing your body to be more receptive to the Holy Spirit.

After Saul of Tarsus experienced his startling revelation of Jesus and was blinded, he was brought to Damascus. "And for three days he was without sight, and neither ate nor drank" (Acts 9:9).

The people in the biblical age fasted and tore their clothes during troubled times. David fasted while his tiny son by Bathsheba lay dying.

"So many cases have come to my attention where fasting has immediately preceded miraculous healing, that there can be no doubt that the denial of the body makes us singularly receptive to the Holy Spirit."*

Sandra Ghost, writing in *Guideposts*, observes:

*Neal, *A Reporter Finds God.*

Along with my Bible searching, I learned from experienced people that not only was fasting an expected part of the God-centered life in biblical times but that many churches had practiced it with varying emphasis ever since. What was new, I found, was the growing use of fasting today by people of all faiths as a normal part of the life of prayer. . . .

In my case, if I've fasted longer than one day and become either weak or hungry, I personally conclude that the Holy Spirit has withdrawn his support for this particular effort. Were I to continue then, it would become a matter of gritted teeth and "works."

Yet under certain circumstances, our hunger can be a sacrifice offered to God.

Medically speaking, prolonged fasts (more than five days) are considered harmful, for it is believed that after a time the body begins to consume its vital organs. Some people fast throughout the day, others several days, while some people simply miss a meal before the healing service. I find that when I am praying for someone who is in critical need, a twenty-four-hour fast is especially meaningful. I do take water or weak tea, however.

5. Repentance, Praise, Thanksgiving

Men suffer for sin, for there is no such thing as sinning without suffering. Even God cannot free us from suffering from sin if we persist in it. But God does not send the suffering. (Of course, it is true that much of human sickness and suffering are due more to the collective sins of our society than to individual sin.)

The Reverend Alfred William Price, who has conducted a healing mission for years in Philadelphia, comments: "Evil thoughts, selfish thoughts, revengeful thoughts, vicious thoughts always cause suffering not only for the individual himself but for others also."

Jesus warns: "If you are offering your gift at the altar, and there remember that your brother has something against you, leave your gift there before the altar and go; first be reconciled" (Matt. 5:23–24).

When we rid ourselves of those grudges and feelings of ill will we hold against certain individuals we will be far more receptive to receive the power of the Holy Spirit. This is one reason why most churches have a "general confession" as part of the liturgy; during this time we should think carefully about our relationships with other people. God forgives us, always. Do we really forgive others? True forgiveness is not an easy step to take.

What is interesting about the healing process is that when healed, often a person changes his way of life. He may give up smoking, or drinking excessively, or being intolerant or cranky.

And what a natural reaction it is to offer up praise and thanksgiving to God when we have been helped by him! One of the characteristics of the Jesus people is that the words "Praise God" come easily to their lips. It is a wonderful way to greet Good News and to thank God.

The story in Luke 17, when ten lepers were healed, illustrates how few people remember to thank God. Thanking God should be a normal part of our lives, thanking him for everything: for our food, friendships, a good sleep, for times of trial when he is instructing us, for radiant sunrises and clear skies, for the work we have to do.

6. Corporate Power of Prayer

We nourish and strengthen one another. When we are alone the night somehow seems darker and the time slower. And it is this way with illness and healing. It is true that healing can take place where only two or three are together, or when an individual is alone. But there is a special sense of power when many come together to share God's love and their own faith. We are human and sometimes our faith wavers. When this happens we can "borrow" the faith of someone else. There is an aura to a healing service that draws us to the center where Christ waits for us.

Jesus emphasized strongly two vital factors in the healing process: faith on the part of the sick man and of those in sympathy with him, and earnest corporate cooperation of all concerned in the effort to bring about a cure.

The six foregoing conditions are in no way inclusive or exclusive. They are simply attributes that most often seem to be a part of the Divine Healing process; they may offer at least a possible answer to those who have not been materially helped.

Sometimes we forget that doctors and nurses are instruments of

God's healing powers. His gift of medical knowledge to us is part of Divine Healing. And frequently doctors will acknowledge that a difficult situation that turned out well could only be due to God's guidance.

Recently I received a letter from a minister who expressed concern about those who are *not* healed, medically or otherwise: "What do we do with the divided parish—the disappointed souls who do not get the healing they have been led to expect?"

This so often appears to be a heartbreaking puzzle, and though there are no *easy* answers, there *are* answers.

First, we know now of these six conditions that are involved to some degree with each individual healing. These conditions are vitally important to maintain both by the one who is ministering and by the suppliant.

Second, though we may be unaware of it at the time, a healing process might be taking place at the core of our inner self. Obviously we cannot know the mind of God in every detail, but we do know that he wills us good. If we allow his will to work in us, we are going to be touched by him in whatever way is most profitable to us at that time. I recall one person saying: "Had I received my physical healing immediately, I don't think I would have felt that need or would have been so eager to go deeper into the ways of God."

There can be a purpose to pain and suffering. I know that in my own life I can state unconditionally that my greatest moments of insight and awareness have been achieved during painful trials. If you put yourself in God's hands he will not fail you. But to get you out of the mess you have made, he may have to lead you along a rocky and painful path.

The point is that no one leaves a healing service untouched by God, though we may not understand initially in just which way we have been reached. Even if someone is not visibly cured, if he will allow it to happen, God draws him closer to Himself.

We are awed by physical healings. We ought to be much more impressed when a person is "turned" toward God, when he is converted, for in this he is turning to eternal things. One's body is here for only a short time.

Dean Chattin told me of a young woman who is virtually blind. Though the healing services have not returned her sight, she has allowed the Holy Spirit to work through her so that people actually envy her joyous approach to life. She has been instrumental in bringing many people back into the Church. She is truly a channel of God's love. At this time in her life she is expressing his will. It may be that she will be healed physically at some future point.

If we go to God in faith, if we ask in the name of Jesus whatever it is we need, we shall receive what is for our good.

Physical death at the proper time is no evil. We know that we have God's promise that through Christ's resurrection we go on to a greater life.

In all our prayers we must remember that we are offering our hearts, our minds, our souls, *and* our bodies for God's use. We ask in the Lord's prayer that *his* will be done, not ours but his. We may find that God has a different, and in the long run a better, answer for him and for us. It is a wonderful thing to feel physically healthy. But it is sublime to be filled with the joy that can come only from God.

CHAPTER EIGHT

Living in Community

We've heard much about communes in recent years. All kinds. On the one hand, we've read about demonic ones; on the other, communities that are distinctively Christian.

The rediscovery of community life is a return to a basic fact of human existence. We are created for community. Within it we learn to be human. We begin in the family. The wider and more open the family the better. At its best it includes grandparents, retired aunts, and passing relatives. From these we move out through our peer groups to enjoy the wider community of human beings.

Through participation in the existence of a community some people are hoping to recover their human dignity. This dignity is the gift of our loving Father. Christ died so that people would become his kinsmen. The family of God, therefore, is the ultimate expression of what we mean when we talk about communes, or communities.

It is perhaps easier to illustrate this truth than to philosophize about it. Toward the end of World War II, a psychiatrist was deeply moved by what he had heard about Nazi concentration camps in Germany. When the first camp was liberated, he met with its victims. After he told them about some of the problems they would have to overcome as the consequence of their long and harsh years of confinement, he suggested that those who were interested in working toward full health should form a community. One was formed and he was asked to be its consultant.

In this community each member was free to express his wishes and to contribute to the well-being of the community as a whole. It was agreed that the community should not live behind walls, but should roam the countryside as it saw fit. It moved from prison bars to the freedom of space—to mountaintops, forests, plains, ocean beaches, and fields. A large mansion was offered to them. It was accepted only when the community members agreed that it would be helpful in sheltering them from winter storms. No records were to be kept, no laws written out, no bells to be rung, and no timetables maintained.

The important thing was that each individual was free to be him or herself. He or she was accepted in love whether happy or sad, angry or anxious, cooperative or withdrawn. Healing took place in fellowship.

This is a model of what community is all about. We are created for fellowship with God and each other. In this fellowship we are accepted as we are without judgment. The testimony of the crucifixion is that we are loved, sins and all. We are accepted into the community of God and his people.

Koinonia as the Basis of Community

Koinonia is a Greek word used in the New Testament that is sometimes translated as community. But it doesn't mean a *group* of people; it means *fellowship.* Sharing life together. Participating in the divine life. Being in communion with God, Christ, and the Holy Spirit. It is the power of spirit that makes the ultimate experience of community possible.

Koinonia is in Christ. It continues through the activity of the Holy Spirit.

Our Lord Jesus Christ brings us into fellowship with our Father and his children in the power of the Holy Spirit. This is the reality that no human organization can duplicate. Without Christ in the midst there is no koinonia and, therefore, no possibility of authentic community. Many a well-intentioned group of people have come together to share a common life only to find that there isn't a power in the group great enough to transcend the fears, anxieties, jealousies, and hang-ups of the group as a whole. Prophets such as Karl Marx, Sigmund Freud, and B. F. Skinner lack such power to the bitter disappointment of many who have tried to follow their teachings.

We may divide our spiritual journey into three stages:

1. Our existence in the mass where we are controlled by the natural, social, political, and psychological orders. Here we trust collective bodies such as the State too much. The more we trust them the greater our sense of frustration and alienation.

2. Our awareness of ourselves as individuals. By rebelling against the controls of our environment we may gain a sense of internal authority. We may become conscious that the "I" who questions, thinks, doubts, suffers, experiences is the only power that affirms life. This sense of individual power may become demonic when it worships itself as the center of existence. This leads to the superman complex of dictators, and many popular politicians.

3. For those who are becoming Christians, the individual's awareness is centered not upon himself, but upon Christ. His freedom is because of him. It is therefore *responsive* and *responsible*. It is freedom in love, for love, to love. It leads to koinonia, the ultimate reality of fellowship in the love of the Holy Spirit.

In describing the spiritual movement of the individual into the joy of fellowship I have used the words *responsive* and *responsible*. These indicate our personal Yes to the call of the Holy Spirit and the acceptance of our accountability for our own actions. Paul sums up the nature of this responsibility in these phrases: "The only thing that counts is faith active in love" (Gal. 5:5, NEB); "Help one another to carry these heavy loads, and in this way you will fulfill the law of Christ" (Gal. 6:2, NEB).

It is obvious from this understanding of fellowship that no one may go it alone. To be a Christian is to be in fellowship. As our sense of *response* and *responsibility* deepens, it also widens to include others without prejudgment in the same manner that our Father's love reaches out through his Son to include his enemies. All of us are in this category at some time or another.

Koinonia is individual and universal. It is also particular and practical. It is sacramental. It is experienced at the moment and point where spirit infuses time and place, and therefore involves our participation in life. In this sense James writes: "The kind of religion which is without stain or fault in the sight of God our Father is this: to go to the help of orphans and widows in their distress and keep oneself untarnished by the world" (James 1:27, NEB).

This particularity, this practicality of love in action is often misunderstood. Because it is, there has been a growing interest in oriental religions among some Americans. While we may learn from these religions, we may never believe that they can replace the Christian faith.

Writing of one type of oriental religion, Albert Schweitzer says: "It is a poverty stricken religion. Its god is mere empty spirituality. Its last word to man is absolute negation of life and of the world. Its ethical content is meagre. It is a mysticism which makes man lose his individual existence in a god that is dead."*

What matters to us when we are ill is that someone nurses us, when we are in prison that someone visits us, when we are lonely that someone loves us, when we are dying that someone comforts us.

This judgment upon communities was given by Jesus: "You have my Father's blessing; come, enter, and possess the kingdom that was made. For when I was hungry, you gave me food; when thirsty, you gave me drink; when I was a stranger you took me into your home; when naked you clothed me; when I was ill you came to my help; when in prison you visited me" (Matt. 25:34–36, NEB).

The Work of the Holy Spirit

The fellowship in which we know the fullness of life is the work of the Holy Spirit. His work is love. When we experience the beauty of being loved we are moved to say, "Yes! Yes, this is what life is all about. Yes, this is what matters supremely." When we do this we are following our heart and intuition.

The fellowship of the Holy Spirit is the Church; the Greek word is *ecclesia*. It means a *gathering* or *congregation* of people. To understand it in the New Testament sense is to know it as the community of faith which shares in the new life of the spirit, inherits the promises of God to Israel, worships Jesus as Christ or Lord, and proclaims the Good News of God's active love. As Christians, we are in the Church. We *are* the Church.

Karl Barth provides us with an interesting commentary on the

Christianity and the Religions of the World (London: Allen & Unwin, 1924).

desertion of the disciples at Gethsemane and Golgotha. He declares that they were not the first Church. Instead, it was the two revolutionaries who were crucified with Jesus:

They crucified him with the criminals. Do you know what this implies? Don't be too surprised if I tell you that this was the first Christian fellowship, the first certain, indissoluble, and indestructible Christian community. Christian community is manifest wherever there is a group of people close to Jesus who are with him in such a way that they are directly and unambiguously affected by his promise and assurance. These may hear that everything he is, he is for them, and everything he does, he does for them. To live by this promise is to be a Christian community.*

Barth may seem to be too harsh in his judgment of the disciples. If so, it is because he is affirming the essential truth of the Church. Christ is its life. The disciples, who had known Jesus in the most intimate of fellowships, had turned away from him. The two victims of crucifixion, however, were with him, one on either side. Where our Lord is with his people, there is his Church.

The point is: It is Jesus our Lord who created the Church. Beside him our bishops, elders, deacons, and ministers pale into insignificance. The miracle of the Church is that it exists despite us. Whenever the love of Christ burns in the heart of a man, there is the Church. And none of us is good enough to say: "This kind of Church isn't good enough."

In the light of this understanding the most helpful image of the Church is that of the body of Christ.

The Body of Christ

Our Lord called his Church into existence when he was in the flesh. He died for it. He also died for the whole of mankind. In Christ, God took the burden of human sin upon his shoulders and his heart. He liberated us from that burden to set us free to be his beloved children. All this was done in the body. In the atoning work of our Lord, our common humanity is taken into this body and transcended, made holy. By faith we respond to *Jesus,* the body

**Deliverance to the Captives* (London: S.C.M. Press, 1961).

crucified and risen, not to an idea about him.

When our Lord rose from the tomb, he rose in two bodies: his new, glorified, and exalted body and the new body of his believers. This new corporate body is the representative of the new redeemed humanity.

Through the saving work of our Lord, the new Humanity is in existence. We see and experience it as the Church or body of Christ. That is, our fellowship is one and visible. It is actual, particular, and practical.

In 1 Corinthians 12 and Romans 12 we have a thoughtfully worked-out doctrine of the Church as the body: "For Christ is like a single body with its many limbs and organs, which many as they are, together make up one body. For indeed we were all brought into one body by baptism, in the one spirit" (1 Cor. 12:12–13, NEB).

As the body of Christ, the *Church is one.* To say this is to be thankful. It is also to be sad. The reality we have been given has been distorted by those who have lacked the humility to let Christ be Lord. Sometimes the Church has been too like the State. It has tried to use its forms, systems, and methods in order to express its practical role.

Where once the Church was a unity, where once it was universal, now it is divided because of our human frailties.

Despite the man-made ordinances that have created the different sects that divide us and prevent us from sharing the one loaf on the Holy Table, we may still affirm our spiritual, personal, and physical unity by worshiping with our fellow Christians whenever we can regardless of the label that may be hung outside the building.

When we worship in spirit and in truth we worship our Father in the power of the one spirit and in the one body of Christ. There is one Church in heaven and on earth. The invisible Church is the continuation of the one Church on earth. It participates in the fullness of the resurrection.

The Body Is One Because Christ Is the Head

The new man, or new humanity, is one because our Lord is at its heart or center. We have mentioned earlier that the closer we come to the center, the closer we come to one another. By ourselves we are broken and fragmented. We are torn apart by many conflicting loyalties. In Christ we are brought together. We see life through his eyes. Suffer with him in the suffering of others. Share in his love as we love his kinsmen. Dietrich Bonhoeffer writes about the Christ in our own heart being weak, but the Christ in the heart of our brother being strong. Therefore, we need our brother.*

In the One Body There Are Many Members

Because the unity of the body is that of the spirit rather than of the law, the uniqueness of each member is honored. Each person has a unique gift of the spirit to donate to the well-being of the body as a whole. This encourages a richness of diversity and a situation where we are free to grow in love. The model of the liberated victims of the Nazi concentration camp that I gave at the beginning of the chapter is an excellent example of what Paul means when he exhorts us to "love one another with brotherly affection; outdo one another in showing honor" (Rom. 12:10).

When I think of how Christ has come to me I have to think of the workingmen, housewives, artists, musicians, stone masons, architects, writers, poets, actors, theologians, philosophers, farmers, sailors, fishermen, preachers, martyrs, saints, children, scientists, carpenters, teachers, students, friends, scholars, doctors, nurses, plumbers, porters, sextons, cooks, waitresses, and prisoners through whom he has come.

I remember one time when there was a flooding tragedy in a nearby town. The members of a church received the news on a Saturday afternoon. By that evening the church had an emergency team of doctors, nurses, and technicians on the spot and had provided homes for all the homeless. On Sunday afternoon a convoy of cars, buses, and trucks loaded with tools, blankets, clothing, medical supplies, and food arrived. It was the Church in action!

As a member of the body of Christ in prison camp I preached, taught, and massaged wasted muscles. Others healed, prayed, made wooden legs for the limbless, created a university, synthesized healing drugs, invented anesthetics, composed verse, sang songs, danced, de-

Life Together (New York: Harper & Row, 1954).

vised and played musical instruments, and broke bread together. This is the miracle that is happening in the world all the time. The endless range of gifts of the spirit are being used in the body.

In our time we are challenged to recover the whole of life for Christ. This can be done only by members of the one body who use their gifts for the exaltation of the head of the body and the edification of their fellow members.

The Body Is Visible

The body of Christ in the world is visible in its compassionate activities. Its love is revealed by its concern for the least of Christ's brethren. These activities, it must be remembered, are not according to regulations. They are the fruits of love. As love wells up from the deep and silent spring of the divine-human fellowship, it expresses itself spontaneously, so spontaneously that the body doesn't remember when it fed the hungry or liberated the captive. In its love for Christ it works for him without thought of praise or reward. He reaches out through the different members to perform his healing ministry gently and graciously.

It is also visible in its worship. Its liturgy is its reasonable service. In the service of God the body is prepared for the service of the world. The world is the garden that men have transformed into a wilderness and that God transforms back into a garden by the careful stewardship of his caring children.

The reformers spoke of the marks of the Church as right preaching of the Word, right celebration of the sacraments, and right discipline. These are the visible marks that identify the body of Christ as being different from and other than the world in which it witnesses.

The worship centers, sanctuaries, chapels, or cathedrals are not the Church, but simply the home of the Church. Because the Church is a body, it needs a place to bring it together, and a time to meet. Those who condemn the 11 A.M. Sunday service fail to realize that worship is the body's business. It gathers, then disperses, to serve.

The body is seen as it listens to the Word. The Word of the Old Covenant, epistles, and Gospels doesn't change. It is timeless. I imagine it is a rare experience to hear that same word on a golf course, in a supermarket, at the movies, or in a Playboy club.

You can, of course, stay in bed and read the same lesson that will be read in the home of the body. But it isn't the same. The Word to be spoken has also to be heard. It is a human activity of the whole body. You may not realize it at first but something is happening when the Word is proclaimed and heard. Our Father who spoke through the body of his Son still speaks to the body that is one in the Holy Spirit. *Listening* is the preparation for proclamation. If the body doesn't take time to listen, the world will have nothing to hear. That is, if the body doesn't listen to the Word it won't have a word to say that differs from the cacophony of the cocktail party chatter.

"But I don't like the preacher," you may say. "He isn't good enough." Of course he isn't. He's like you. No one is good enough. He may not be as clever as you, nor as witty, or wealthy, or handsome, or as well dressed, or as important. Yet, for all his faults, he is a member of the one body. For all his shortcomings, he has been entrusted to handle holy things. He has been set apart as one of the "stewards of the mysteries of God" (1 Cor. 4:1). He is part of the earthen vessel that exists to hold the treasure of the Gospel.

I once had supper with a group of people who were tearing the minister apart because he wasn't as popular as a famous musical group, as successful as a well-known preacher and writer, or as entertaining as a television personality. This cannibalism was suddenly brought to a halt by a beautiful old lady who said strongly and clearly: "Pardon my interruption, but I think you are all talking nonsense. Of course, he isn't all the things you say he should be. He wouldn't be a minister if he were. Whatever he is, no one has more to give than he has. Suppose someone were to hand you a check for a fortune. Would you say, 'I don't like his looks. His suit is badly fitting. His voice is terrible?' You know you wouldn't. You'd be so busy thanking him you wouldn't give a damn what he looked like. Why don't you do the same to the poor minister you've cut up into shreds. He's handing you the biggest check of all—the Gospel. Listen to him for a change instead of to yourselves. Try saying, 'Thank you, for the Gospel.' "

She's right. "So faith comes from what is heard, and what is heard comes by the preaching of Christ" (Rom. 10:17). In the preaching of Christ the proclaimer becomes "God's sacrament to men." The Word came through him. It may only be effective when we take the time to be attentive. For the Word to be rightly preached it must be rightly listened to by the rest of the body.

The mark of discipline is natural to anybody. It is not a matter of punishment but of learning and understanding. It is learning in love through love.

We learn, therefore, from the attitudes of our fellow members. Whatever part we have to perform, we can do so because of others. When the mouth speaks, the ears listen. When a nerve sends a signal, the toe bends. The members are sensitive to us and our needs. By their attitudes we know them. There was a time, remember, when the pagan world said of the body: "See how these Christians love one another!"

One place where twentieth-century pagans can see this love is in Christian communities. It is important to differentiate between Christian communities and communes. A commune or a community is composed of a group of people who have agreed to live together and to share what they have. Though they come in all sizes, shapes, and forms, they generally fall into three classifications.

1. Some are spontaneous, and they disappear just about as fast as they appear. Usually they are made up of people who come together haphazardly to share companionship. These communes are almost always disorganized, unsanitary, sexually permissive, and a far cry from the utopia that was dreamed of. They disappoint because there is no sense of real love, peace, or of unity. For most participants they are no solution at all, and for some the experience is a real disaster.

2. Another group are those non-Christian communes founded either by a "guru" or on an idea, such as getting back to nature. In the latter group land is the all-important thing. Communes like these may or may not last depending on the sense of organization and the overall philosophy. The Wheeler Ranch in California, for example, is a typical farming, back-to-nature operation and has become quite well known. Those groups resembling it are successful because they are based on realistic principles of sharing a work load and a spirit of cooperation. But "love money"—money from relatives and friends—is usually necessary to keep them going.

The communes built around personality cults gradually dissolve or turn into something completely undesirable, sometimes demonic. It is tragic how young people searching for The Way unwittingly become trapped into what at first looks like a spiritually worthwhile venture.

3. Christian communities have the longest life span because Christ is the center. The whole sense of such a community is that of a large family, for the members think of themselves as being "brothers and sisters in Christ."

These communities are usually well organized and clean. The work load is more evenly distributed. The emphasis is on the life of the spirit rather than on material things. All resources are pooled. Even if none are affluent, nonetheless those that I am aware of have always had three meals a day. No one has gone hungry, though the menu in lean times is apt to become monotonous. Yet the young people are unusually resourceful in making their food tasty. Guests—and there are plenty of them—are never turned away. "We want to be like a church. If we have it good, we have a responsibility to the world to help out. If that means giving somebody a meal or some inspiration or to tell him about Jesus, we try."

Most Christian communes have married couples as well as single people. There is no promiscuity. Since they attempt to guide their lives by the New Testament, they take Christ's words and Paul's teachings at face value.

Meals especially seem to be times of warm fellowship, and there is an easy, quiet joy reflected in this simple, sharing life. They always remember to thank God who does not fail to supply them with what they need. There are regular times for Bible study, alone and with a group. Members are genuinely polite with one another and frequently you hear someone say: "Yeah, I never thought of looking at it that way." Children have the advantage of a larger "family" to play with and a home life that has that atmosphere of a happy playground.

An active community will have many visitors, some badly strung-out on drugs. And it is here that the most beautiful and loving witnessing takes place. You can feel the Holy Spirit at work. In contrast to most other non-Christian communes, there is a very definite sense of discipline and orderly thinking based on trying to practice the presence of Christ.

The Christian communities seem to be fulfilling a need that some people have to live together as a "family." In our rather detached society these communities provide a sense of belonging, of not being separated, of knowing that you are loved for yourself alone and not what you might represent as a member of society. There is a growing trend for young people to gather together in communities and their example may be helpful to others who are searching for a better way of life.

With T. S. Eliot we may recite:

> What life have you if you have not life together?
> There is no life that is not in community,
> And no community not lived in praise of God.
> —From "Choruses from *The Rock*"

CHAPTER NINE

How To Care for Friends and Relatives When Only You Have Been Converted

You know you have turned from darkness to light, from an old way of life to a new, from the tyranny of the self to the freedom of Christ. How do you tell your friends or parents about it? You could come home one day and say enthusiastically: "The best thing has happened to me! I've become a Christian."

In saying this you could be welcomed with joy and find you are free to share your faith with the other members of your household. If this is your situation, you are blessed.

You may, however, have announced your new identity in Christ only to be treated with indifference or hostility.

An undergraduate visited me before Christmas vacation of his senior year and announced that he was going home to tell everybody he was a Christian and that he was going to study for the ministry. After the holiday I asked him: "How did your announcement fare?" He laughed, "It's taken me time to work that out. When I told my parents, they were pleased. My friends, particularly my girl friends, thought I had flipped my lid. Then they thought I was being funny. When I told my parents I was planning to go to seminary, they didn't think it was such a good idea. They suggested I go into business. I'd be more effective there, and," here his smile widened, "I'd make a lot more money. My girl friends went wild. They hated the idea of the ministry. It wasn't for people who live in the suburbs and belong to the country club."

Your experience may be similar to this. Or it may be worse. Some parents have remarked that there was something spooky about conversion. Maybe their son or daughter needed psychiatric help. It would be more normal to be turned on to drugs, or sex, or SDS. But Jesus? Help!

One wife said of her husband, "How could he be doing a thing like this to me? Of all things, Christianity! It's weird. How can I face my friends? What can I tell them? He was such a nice guy when I married him."

You may have experienced indifference or hostility. It is sometimes hard to know which is worse. Whatever, it is a time of testing for you, a time when your ego is on the witness stand. We naturally seek its good and it glorification. We want other people to praise us and speak kindly of us. It is hard to lose their approval. We are tempted to feel hurt, then angry. In our anger we condemn them for not appreciating our new condition. We could hardly call anger the evidence of a new and better life.

We might feel ourselves to be so right and our relatives so wrong that we are tempted to browbeat them into accepting our view of God. One way of doing this might be that of saying; "I'm converted, and you're not. You'll go to hell. I won't." It is doubtful if either of these expressions would help them or ourselves.

Once I was traveling on the top of a double-decker bus with a girl friend on our way to a walk in the country. We were happy and enjoying our youth. A man in a dark grey business suit passed us and handed us a tract, asking us if we were saved. He didn't say from what or for what. We looked at the tract. In smudgy black capital letters it told us to flee the wrath to come. Instead of interesting and involving us in the Good News, he left us with the feeling that religion was grey, joyless, depressing, and antilife. This type of approach has made atheists rather than converts of thousands.

The news of our conversion has to be shown as well as declared. This calls for a new attitude, one in which our ego is not sitting stridently on its throne demanding that everyone pay it homage. Remember, your life has a new center. We need to remember this hourly as well as daily. Christ is at the center. He is king. The closer we are to him the closer we come to each other.

In order to let Christ reign as Lord in our lives, it helps to realize that we are not on our own, isolated in the prison of our ego. We have been set free. In our freedom we can hardly be expected to rant and rave. On the contrary. The experience of liberation or salvation is similar to that written about by Siegfried Sassoon in his poem "Everyone Sang":

> Everyone suddenly burst out singing;
> And I was filled with such delight
> As prisoned birds must find in freedom,
> Winging wildly across the white
> Orchards and dark green fields; on, on,
> and out of sight.

Our new freedom is demonstrated in a new attitude, one that becomes more like that of Jesus when he said: "For the Son of man also came not to be served but to serve, and to give his life as a ransom for many" (Mark 10:45). This new attitude is described by Paul as the new mind: "Have this mind among yourselves, which you have in Christ Jesus, who, though he was in the form of God, did not count equality with God a thing to be grasped, but emptied himself, taking the form of a servant" (Phil. 2:5–7). In this attitude of serving rather than being served we are in a better condition to tell of our new allegiance.

Recognize the Difference

To help your self-understanding, take time to recognize the difference between your old and new beings.

Your list of priorities is different. Your commitment to Christ is the decision that shapes all your other decisions. They are now more for him and less for yourself. You don't have to be "hassled" about being the center of everyone's attention. You can think of others for a change. You can look them in the face as the beloved sisters or brothers for whom Christ died. You have no need to compete with others, or to tell lies in order to pretend that you are a better person than you think you are.

This is the key. You are free to be your good and bad self. You are free, therefore, to be sincere. At one time, when a person bought a sculptor's work of art he would test it with a knife to make sure that defects in carving had not been covered over with beeswax or a similar substitute. A pure piece of art was *sincerus,* free from impurities or pretence.

J. B. Phillips translates the sixth beatitude as: "Blessed are the sincere, for they shall see God." Our sincerity is the difference that is either a witness to, or a judgment upon, the world. Reluctant though we are to be different from our friends, we cannot avoid it if we are to be sincere with ourselves before God. Sincerity of this nature is our response to the demand of God as it is expressed by the Psalmist:

> Who shall ascend the hill of the Lord?
>   And who shall stand in his holy place?
> He who has clean hands and a pure heart,
>   who does not lift up his soul to what is false,
>   and does not swear deceitfully (Ps. 24:3–4).

Our sincerity may not assure us of acceptance, but it will save us from swearing deceitfully. We cannot swear loyalty to Mammon (material things) and Christ at the same time.

We have a different destination from the old world we have left behind. The new end is not a safe place in the city and a comfortable house in the suburbs; it is the Kingdom of God and his righteousness. This end enables us to keep everything else in perspective. It makes our list of priorities clear.

Your family and friends may rightly expect to see evidence of the new you. The first laugh that expressed the acceptance of your news could be the laughter of uncertainty. Laughter can cover a wide range of complex emotions. It may be transformed into a smile of thankfulness.

Our new attitude is the most effective, indeed, the only valid witness we may bear. Our sincerity will show by the way we care, which is revealed in our day-to-day relationships. If we care, we are unlikely to become angry with members of our household for expecting us to take our fair share of family chores. Washing the supper dishes and Bible study are not inconsistent. We have read of how our Lord washed his disciples' feet. Our faith does not provide us with excuses but with the means of overcoming the world.

The following extract from a letter illustrates the frustration of a husband who feels that he has lost his wife rather than being blessed with a new woman in Christ: "She accompanies me to church but only as a lost convert or a worldly backslider. I am now merely a humdrum and well-meaning church Christian to her. My wife is God-inspired all day long, and no nun at confessional gives more implicit obedience to her father confessor than she does to the guidance of her leader. I am in serious danger of having all my family torn up by the roots by this wife with whom I have lived for twenty-four years. She is the prize convert of the group. . . . It is my domestic peace and home life that is destroyed—nay, even wrecked, seemingly beyond repair, revision, or restoration."

I interpret this letter as a cry from the heart. The husband was not hostile to her conversion. He was sympathetic. What worried him was that his wife cut him out of her life. She didn't seem to care. She was so busy praying for his conversion, perhaps, that she had no time left to expect an answer. She may have been so busy about her new religion that she had no time left over for living it.

This is a common fault. We may become so involved in the peripheral trappings of faith that we lose its substance. Luke gives a good example of this in Acts 12. Herod had put Peter in prison and a group of believers met to pray for him. Their prayers were answered. He was released miraculously and went to the house of John Mark's mother where the prayer meeting for him was being held. He knocked at the door. Rhoda answered. She was so happy at seeing Peter that she ran to tell the "pray-ers." They turned, annoyed by her enthusiastic intrusion, and admonished her: "You are mad." They prayed for Peter and refused to believe the answer when it came.

We do the same thing. We trust our methods too much and God too little. We nurse our hurts and forget to heal. We tell God what to do when he has already done it. We hate each other for the love of God.

Being sincere surely means living honestly in the presence of God without wax. Loving him means loving our nearest kin. Isn't this where our love for God begins? With our nigh-dweller, our neighbor. And who is more neighbor than your father, mother, husband, wife, sister, brother? The initiative must be yours, not theirs. You are the one who is converted. You are the one who has to prove your sincerity graciously. Jesus teaches us to go the other mile, to do more than is expected of us. Only you know what the other mile is in your home and home town.

You Are Not Alone

New converts are sometimes arrogant and rude because they assume that they are one person against the world. They aren't!

When we learn to understand the difference between the old and the new way of life, we can realize that we are never alone. That was a characteristic of the old when we were lonely in a crowd and alienated by the materialistic values of society. In our new life we take Christ and his promises seriously. One of them is that he will be with us forever and everywhere. That includes to the ends of the earth and to the end of the age. It also applies to our neighborhood. He is with us now. Where we are.

We don't go it alone. We are with Christ, and his brothers and sisters. For a variety of reasons our good news may be received unkindly. We are hurt. Naturally. We are human. And we are learning an important lesson. If we nurse our resentment, we'll overlook the lesson and miss the glory of our new life in fellowship. Instead of hiding in a corner licking our wounds, we have the privilege of telling our Lord about our complaint. Having done that, be quiet and listen. There is relief in the praying. There is, however, strength in the listening. Someone has said that for each person who says "Speak, Lord, for Thy servant heareth," there are at least ten who cry "Hear, Lord! for Thy servant speaketh." When our flow of words dries up, we are ready to hear the Word. We'll know not only where our friends were wrong, but where we were, and what we ought to do to be right.

We are also free to tell our new brothers. By sharing our problem, we'll be helped, and by listening to the reply, we shall be instructed. Experiences of good or ill are occasions for sharing them. We "give back the life" we owe. In doing so, it becomes richer.

We are not alone in our rejection in our witness. We have the resources of all God's people in every generation at our service. By ourselves we don't have the wit and the knowledge to convince other people. It is doubtful, anyway, if clever arguments have ever won a convert. God cannot be proved like a problem or theory in mathematics. We can, however, show that we care by sharing whatever knowledge or insights we have gained at an appropriate time. It may be at a meal or by the fireside. Someone may have mentioned that the thing they can't stand about Christians is that they take themselves and their faith so seriously. Who are they to think that they are the only ones who have the truth, the whole truth, and nothing but the truth?

There's no need to become aggressively defensive. Agree that Christians aren't the only ones to know the truth. There is only one man who did, and he was crucified. Admit that the Bible doesn't expect us to know the whole truth. We may only know in part. And what we know is only a splinter of the truth known by all God's people. It isn't God who withholds his truth from people; it is people who aren't interested. John tells us, for example, that there is a light that gives light to every man. The light of the world has shone in every generation. That light is Jesus Christ.

Thinkers such as Augustine have written that there has never been a time when the truth didn't exist. This, you remark, seems reasonable. But, as for yourself, you wouldn't know the truth apart from Christ. You know him as the way, the truth, and the life.

Don't expect to win the argument. Leave that to the Holy Spirit.

You may have read a book that expresses your feelings. Tell others about it. A speaker who has enlarged your wisdom may be in town. Invite someone to hear him. There may be a special event at your church. Ask your indifferent relatives or hostile friends to come with you.

The range of truth and its expression is always bigger than your mind. Realize this thankfully, and educate yourself to take advantage of it.

As you allow your faith to open you graciously and compassionately to others, you will find that there are occasions when you may say your word and have it heard. Not only may you invite others to share your insights and concerns, you may share the friendship of your new brothers and sisters in Christ with them. Your relatives may even begin to like them to the extent of listening to the reasons of the hope that is in them. Someone may say: "I like John Brown although he's a Christian. He suggested I should read C. S. Lewis's *Four Loves.* Maybe I'll get it out of the library."

One afternoon two young men came to see me. One said of the other: "We were having a discussion. He says he can't believe anything in the Bible; therefore, he can't see why I could possibly become a Christian. I've invited him to have a go with you. I'l! leave him to you. He's my roommate. He'll tell me how he got on when he comes back." That put me on the spot. The questions he asked, however, were reasonable, and I answered them reasonably. When he returned to his room, he carried on a conversation that resulted, some time later, in conversion.

You Haven't Lost

If you have honestly lived your faith and find that your relations at home are becoming worse, not better, because your fault is that of being a Christian and different from the world, don't give up. Enjoy your new life in the new fellowship of your friends in Christ. At the same time be patient with those at home. You know you can't force them to accept you as you are. You are called to be faithful. Your conversion is still happening. The question you may have to ask yourself from time to time is "What does Christ think of me?" rather than "What do I think about Christ?" Let him win the argument with yourself.

You may be in a situation where the best thing to do is to shake the dust of the place off your feet and go elsewhere. In a fraternity two new Christians indicated that they had been converted. To their astonishment this brought down the wrath of the fraternity house upon them. They were cruelly grilled and ridiculed. They decided a witness was impossible and resigned. Two others, however, learned from their experiences and resigned with them to take up residence together as a group.

We are not defeated by such hostility. The darkness has never loved the light. The Good News we have received is that although the world may give us a hard time, we have every reason to be cheered. Christ has overcome the world.

CHAPTER TEN

How Do You Know God's Will?

The Christian faith has a particular teaching about man. He is flesh, but he is more than flesh. He is influenced by his total environment, yet he is more than his environment. He is the peak of God's creation. But more than that, he is created in the image and likeness of God in order to have fellowship with his creator. Through the creative work of Jesus, the eternal Logos become flesh, those who respond to him are brought into the family of God as his brothers and sisters.

This reduction of the doctrine of man to its simplest terms is essential to our understanding of God and his will. How do we know anyone's will? Not by thinking of it as an abstraction or as the product of reason. We know only by knowing the person. When we describe someone we know well we usually say he is kind, gentle, sensitive, sympathetic, compassionate, understanding, trusting, loyal, honest, sincere, and so on. These adjectives are attempted descriptions of what we call will. We could not know the will of anyone unless we saw it in personal action.

We have already noted how Jesus emphasized the inner life as the watershed of morality. If it is polluted, everything that flows from it will be polluted.

In one of his lessons of the Upper Room, Jesus told his disciples that it was by abiding in him that they would bear much fruit, and therefore prove themselves to be his disciples. The chain of fellowship is clear. The Father loves the Son. The Son loves his disciples. His disciples, in knowing the Son by the manifestation of the Father's will in the flesh, are thus able to know the Father.

By faith we already know the will of God because we respond to it. We now know the Father because we have called his Son Lord in the power of the Holy Spirit. We know the goodness of God's will because we have already experienced it at work in our lives. Because we are human, we can never fully know our Father's will, therefore, we can never speak as God to others. We may only speak as brothers.

Doing God's Will

The emphasis of the Bible is upon doing rather than knowing, for it is in the doing that the truth is known. When Jesus was teaching in the Temple at the time of the Feast of Tabernacles, those who had heard him or heard of him began to argue about him. One group said: "He is a good man." Another denied this on the grounds that he was leading the people astray because of his unorthodox behavior. Yet another questioned his teaching credentials. On hearing of this argument, Jesus said: "My teaching is not mine, but his who sent me; if any man's will is to do his will, he shall know whether the teaching is from God or whether I am speaking on my own authority" (John 7:16–17).

The way to test God's will is to do it. Only then shall we know and know humbly. At the end of Albert Schweitzer's important book, *The Quest of the Historical Jesus,* he writes,

He comes to us as One unknown without a name, as of old, by the lake-side, He came to those men who knew Him not. He speaks to us the same word: "Follow thou me!" and sets us to the tasks which he has to fulfil for our time. He commands. And to those who obey Him, whether they be wise or simple, He will reveal Himself in the toils, the conflicts, the sufferings which they shall pass through in His fellowship, and as an ineffable mystery they shall learn in their own experience *Who* He is."*

To think about "the will of God" is to think in the shadows or to use the term as a substitute for "my will." In Jesus the human and divine will are one as we shall see in the discussion on the meaning of faith. He is the divine will manifest and, at the same time, the

---

**The Quest of the Historical Jesus* (London: Adam & Chas. Black, 1954).

ultimate realization of the human will in response. To know the Father's will, therefore, is first to do it. The Word we obey is the same as the one heard by the first disciples; "Follow thou me!" It is in the following that we know. We follow a person. The one who is "the same yesterday and today and for ever" (Heb. 13:8) is the fact of the eternal will with which we have to deal, the fact who shatters all our theories and all our clever doctrines.

To Do God's Will Is to Follow Christ

There are moments when we want to shout out loudly and clearly: "Yes, yes, Lord I'll follow you—anywhere!" No sooner has the last echo of that "anywhere" died than it becomes a question, *anywhere?* And how do we answer? "Yes, I'll follow you to your glory." And of course, there is glory. The glory of life's fulfillment, the glory of loving fellowship, the glory of life's victory. But wait a moment, aren't you rushing things? Think of what is written: "Let us run with perseverance the race that is set before us, looking to Jesus the pioneer and perfecter of our faith, who for the joy that was set before him"—did what? sat on cloud nine and strummed his harp? No! He "endured the cross, despising the shame" (Heb. 12:1–2).

Doing God's will involves more than a purr of pleasure because we feel a rosy glow in our lower abdomen. All of what we are is involved. Look up the experiences of the would-be disciples in Luke 9:57–62. "I'll follow you anywhere," said a man. Anywhere? Jesus said: "Foxes have holes, and birds of the air have nests; but the Son of man has nowhere to lay his head."

Another man heard Jesus say: "Follow me." But he replied: "Sure, when my father is dead." Another responded with a fussy flourish of his hands and voice: "I will follow you, Lord; but let me first say farewell to those at my home." "My home" could mean lots of things. Some of us never truly leave it. We spend our lives going around saying "farewell." We never leave. We never make it to the frontier with Abraham and the rest. Wasn't much of this implied in Jesus' reply: "No one who puts his hand to the plow and looks back is fit for the kingdom of God."

Make Up Your Mind!

The way Jesus says "Follow me" tells us that although God has given us eternal life, which we share by doing his will, this "doing" demands all of what we are. We must make up our minds and go the whole way. We say good-bye to our home and our buddies and leave them behind forever. We cannot escape the cross. It belongs with the "Follow me!" Jesus never wanted anyone to make the mistake of thinking that he offered an easy way. Listen to him: "For which of you, desiring to build a tower, does not first sit down and count the cost, whether he has enough to complete it? Otherwise, when he has laid a foundation, and is not able to finish, all who see it begin to mock him, saying, 'This man began to build, and was not able to finish.' " (Luke 14:28–30).

And so we have to make up our mind that although we may not have much to give him who has given us so much, he expects all of it. God's will embraces all of our life. We can't say Yes to Jesus and cheat or beat his brethren. We can't hear what Jesus has to say about loving each other and then use one of his family as an object of sexual gratification. We can't keep running away from him to follow some false prophet or fad of the moment.

There's a cost involved. Make up your mind that you sincerely want to do God's will. If you do, the promise is beautiful: "Blessed are those who hunger and thirst for righteousness, for they shall be satisfied."

God's Family

The commitment we make to Christ is made individually. Our following him, however, is in the fellowship of those who seek to do his will every day and in every place. This is the family of God. In any loving family the children delight to do their father's will because they have learned to trust him and to know from personal experience that his will is agape.

The quality of our faithfulness can be tested by our response to the illustration of Jesus about the two sons. When the father told one to do a certain errand, he replied enthusiastically, "Certainly, Dad. There's nothing better I can think of doing." His thinking, alas, was separated from his action and so he failed to do what he had promised. The other son didn't think the chore was worth doing, and told his father so; nevertheless, he ended up doing it. It is the *doing*, Jesus emphasizes: "Not every one who says to me, 'Lord, Lord,' shall enter the kingdom of heaven, but he who does the will of my Father who is in heaven." (Matt. 7:21).

By doing God's will as loving sisters and brothers of Jesus Christ we transcend the limitations of our earthly family. In his providence God has so ordered our existence that we are all part and parcel of the family of man in which we share the solidarity of our humanity. Because of our sin we leave God out and reduce our human solidarity and our family situations to the sorry level of being the expressions of our pride and stupidity. Thus families become the scenes of internecine feuds and battles, and the chaos of Babel rules the destinies of nations.

God's family transcends all these silly limitations we naturally impose upon ourselves. His will for us is that we should be one in the power of his love. The ministry of Jesus in its early stage seems to have been popular with the people. This led to increasing opposition to him on the part of civil and ecclesiastical dignitaries. Rumors were spread indicating that the good he was doing was not really good at all. It was nothing other than the work of Beelzebul, the lord of the underworld.

From the chronological list of events recorded by Mark, we may presume that Mary heard something of these rumors and became anxious about Jesus. She and her sons came to a house in which he was teaching. They sent someone in through the crowd to say that his mother and brothers were outside waiting for him. They may have expected him to stop teaching and come back with them to the old carpenter's shop, and so stay out of trouble. But Jesus replied by saying: "Who are my mother and my brothers?"

Then, looking around those who were present, he stretched out his arms to embrace them, and answered his own question: "Here are my mother and my brothers! Whoever does the will of God is my brother, and sister, and mother" (Mark 3:33–34). These are strong words. Once again we see how Jesus expected all of a person, not part of him, and that the life of full obedience is lived within the family of God. There can be no substitutes. Only when families are themselves within this greater family are they free to overcome the division of our all-too-selfish natural relationships and free to become "a living, loving unity whose harmony is the harmony of heaven and whose peace is the peace of God."

Life in God's family is clearly different from anything we may have been taught in home and Sunday school where we were promised heaven if we did what Mom and the teacher asked. But the will of God is not a dull chore imposed upon us by the patterns of conventional society. It is a passionate response to an absolute demand. What do you make of these words: "If any one comes to me and does not hate his own father and mother and wife and children and brothers and sisters, yes, and even his own life, he cannot be my disciple" (Luke 14:26). We have explained in Chapter 4 that Jesus did not mean dislike. He meant that he must come first in our life. Who could make such a demand except God himself. Our corrupt and polluted culture can hardly be expected to look upon it kindly. We cannot understand Jesus' demand unless, once again, we look at him through whom it comes to us. He is not in our image. He is the active will of God in human form.

Our active participation in God's family as obedient children helps us to understand our Father's will more clearly. Jesus is seen for what he is eternally. As we empty our egos of their hoarded baggage Christ is given more room to enter and be more completely Lord. His will, therefore, becomes increasingly our will, his peace our peace, his joy our joy. Thus the prayer of our heart is like that of the Psalmist: "I delight to do thy will" (Ps. 40:8).

To part of the family of God in Laodicea came these instructions through the revelation of John from the living Christ: "Those whom I love, I reprove and chasten; so be zealous and repent. Behold, I stand at the door and knock; if any one hears my voice and opens the door, I will come in to him and eat with him, and he with me" (Rev. 3:19–20). This is a promise that is regularly fulfilled.

In any reasonably happy family there is a constant sense of activity. Its members agree and disagree with each other. So it is in God's family. Its openness to his will pitches us into an activity of concern, questioning, and probing. Along with Jacob, we have to wrestle with our Father's messengers, or angels, in the night watches until the dawn floods us with light.

Be in His Will

The family of God is the school of obedience in which we learn to do our Father's will. All of us have to begin where we are. That's usually in the nursery. We learn to say honestly: "Not my will, but thine be done." Our thoughts are more centered on our Elder Brother we are learning to love. Because they are, we think more about our brothers and sisters. We remember them in our prayers. Joe has a sick wife, Mary has lost her mother, Ann has money problems, Bill is concerned about his coming session with his draft board because of his claim as a conscientious objector. Mrs. Smith, at the end of the road, will need her driveway shoveled after this snow has fallen; I'd better get there early. The minister asked for volunteers for the Sunday school—that probably means me.

Because we are learners, we shall make mistakes. When we do it is important to remember that God doesn't hold these mistakes against us. He gives us a new chance. We begin again where we left off. We do what we can for our Lord wherever we are. He takes these acts of obedience and uses them for his glory.

The practice of obedience liberates us from the controls of our egos and their loyalty to the world. Paul wrote: "Do not be conformed to this world but be transformed by the renewal of your mind, that you may prove what is the will of God, what is good and acceptable and perfect" (Rom. 12:2).

At the nursery school level we may be disturbed by the sense of conflict we experience. Our old self is back there in Sin City. It keeps telling us not to be fools for Christ's sake, but to be wise with the wisdom of the world and make a fast buck when it comes our way; or not to be so scrupulous about our morals, for all that matters is that we should have fun. We learn by practice. As we do, our wills become more in line with the divine will. We therefore enter more fully into the peace that passes human understanding. That peace is at the center of life where we are in communion with our Father.

T. S. Eliot concludes the story of his spiritual pilgrimage in his poem "Ash Wednesday"·

> Teach us to sit still
> Even among these rocks,
> Our peace in His will.

The "my will" or the "I will" that causes us so much anxiety gives way to the peace and joy of "Thy will be done." This is our experience on the other side of the cross. This is where our Lord leads us, "who for the joy that was set before him endured the cross." In the joy of his presence we know who he is, and we know the tasks he is giving us to complete in our time.

In a conversation with a reporter, Eberhard Bethge, Dietrich Bonhoeffer's biographer, said that the great question of Bonhoeffer's life was "Who is Christ?" In his earlier days, he asked "Who is Christ generally?" Later, he changed the question to "Who is Christ for us today?" This question was more modest than the earlier one. Because it was, it succeeded in showing Bonhoeffer that Christ was not in the skies. He is here in our midst. Through him we know God's will here and now. By following him we do it. Bonhoeffer showed his loyalty to him by bearing a brave witness in Nazi Germany in World War II. Like his master, he knew agony of the cross. But he lived in the power of the resurrection.

CHAPTER ELEVEN

Increasing Your Faith

Faith is not a trip but a journey, a spiritual pilgrimage.
In its own way it is an exploring expedition, for though general maps are available, made by those who have gone before you, and though often you will come across well-traveled paths, there will be times when you will be forging your own way. Each of us is unique. Our approach to God will show some variation. But most travelers send back descriptions that have much in common.

In your pilgrimage you are going to be throwing away a lot of baggage you've accumulated over the years and to which you have become attached. As you climb higher toward the "City of God" you begin to discard certain items that more and more impede your progress: pet peeves, your tendency to shade the truth to yourself and to others, dependence on drugs or alcohol, crankiness, spite, gossiping, self-hatred, too much self-concern, laziness, fornication.

If you are going to continue your journey these things are too much for you to carry, so bit by bit you find yourself getting rid of them. And as you do, you begin to feel freer and lighter. You begin to sense the meaning of real freedom. You are no longer burdened like a slave carrying the devil's pack for him. You begin to feel healthier and you discover yourself. You become more of a unity, less of a mix of disparate parts.

As in any exploration you must follow certain basic guidelines to keep you from being lost. To increase your faith, to draw closer to God, to be in a position to receive the promises of Christ, you will find it necessary to set up a way of life. This will include meditation, prayer, Bible reading and study, as well as being a Christian active in the world.

A mistake many people make, however, is to plunge too quickly and deeply into the spiritual waters before they even know how to dog paddle. A friend of mine came to the religious life via Skid Row as an alcoholic and approached it with sprawling and undirected enthusiasm. Fortunately he had a wise spiritual guide.

"When I first began to listen to this man (the guide), he questioned me about my habits of prayer. 'How long do you go?' he asked. 'About two hours at a stretch,' I said, trying with a violent effort to appear modest. It was true. I was less than twelve months out of moral and physical collapse in which I had been floundering for years. But I had been reading books, and I am a Rover Boy at heart, and I *was* practicing, at that time, two hours at a clip."

"My old spiritual father looked at me narrowly. 'You do this every day?' he asked."

" 'Well, no,' I replied."

" 'You do it for a few days and then skip a few days?' "

" 'Yes,' I said."

" 'And sometimes you skip a few weeks, perhaps?' "

" 'That's the way it goes,' I said."

" 'Ten minutes a day for you,' he ordered. 'No *more* and no *less.*' "

"Thank God I found my way into the old man's hands. In another few months I probably would have blown some fuses or soured myself on prayer for evermore the way I was going."*

And so I pass along the same good advice to you. In the beginning practice five minutes of meditation and five minutes of prayer each and every day without fail. As it becomes a habit and you feel more comfortable, increase the time according to your capacity. You will know when the time is right.

*Thomas E. Powers, *First Questions on the Life of the Spirit* (New York; Harper & Row, 1959).

Meditation

Meditation is essentially holding before the mind one idea that you examine carefully. As you reflect on a particular subject, other ideas related to it will develop. The problem is always to keep your meditations within the limit of your main idea.

Zen, which has enjoyed something of a vogue in the West, is based on meditation. It is through an intensely disciplined meditation that one is led to *satori*, enlightenment.

Meditation does not have to be of a religious nature. I know a successful Greek businessman who gets up an hour before breakfast and with cigarettes and coffee meditates on his business. I have sat on my farm tractor in the midst of a golden fall afternoon completely caught up in the ineffable beauty. Meditation about this miracle of nature is a natural reaction.

Transcendental meditation, promulgated by Maharishi Mahesh Yogi of India, is not necessarily religiously oriented. One adherent described her state: "My mind became blank as a scrubbed-down blackboard as I began to repeat silently my "mantra," a meaningless syllable from ancient Sanskrit that is supposed to help your mind transcend all thought to a blissful state of pure consciousness."

In this book, however, meditation will be regarded in a religious sense as being one of the spokes of a wheel leading to the hub, God.

Meditation should not be confused with daydreaming, when you might envision yourself as a famous artist or the star quarterback or think randomly about last year's vacation. Meditation is disciplined thinking. It is pondering a subject deeply. Because meditation is a sensitizing process it opens you to an entirely new dimension of experience, giving you insights you would never have had otherwise. You are no longer looking at things on the surface.

One of the difficulties, especially in the beginning, is that your mind is the respository of everything you have seen, heard, or read. Consequently, millions of thoughts are on tap. Your problem is to direct and to select the flow.

Selecting a regular time and place is helpful. I have found that before breakfast works out best for me, but this is not always feasible for others. Housewives, for example, may have children and husbands to get off to school and work. Choose the period of the day that will give you uninterrupted moments.

A woman in California lives with her family on a small sailing boat. Privacy is at a premium. I suggested that she lock herself in the head (bathroom to landlubbers) to be alone. When you know that a door may be opened or someone might speak to you, your warning system is keeping you alert on the surface of things, and you will not be able to withdraw to the deep privacy of yourself. Jesus advises: "When you pray, go into your room and shut the door" (Matt. 6:6). With practice, though, you may do this even in the crowded subway trains and traffic jams when you have no opportunity to be alone.

You should be comfortable but alert. The reason to be comfortable is that you do not want to be aware of your body. Being comfortable does not mean lounging. When you slump in a chair your body is under actual tension. The muscles are working against each other.

I have found two positions comfortable and effective.

Sit in a straight-backed chair, both feet on the floor, hands resting in the lap, back and head erect. Your total bodily sensation is much like the advice tennis teachers give to students: "Your grip must be firm, but your arm relaxed." It sounds like a contradiction in terms. You are relaxed, but like an apparently dozing cat ready to pounce on an idea.

The other position I like is to sit cross-legged either on the floor with my back supported against something firm or on a couch that is not too soft. This is a quasilotus position.

The secret of a successful meditation is to choose a subject that has real meaning for you. I find that my meditations are best when they center around a specific point. I have studied the psalms extensively and I often take a passage that strikes me as being pertinent to my needs. I use the Gospels and Epistles in the same way and frequently a book of devotions. It is important to be specific, otherwise your mind will be as capricious as a leaf caught in a wind. Gradually I find it begins to center on the topic. I think carefully about it. As might be expected, at times I am taken along unexpected paths.

One of the soundest means of making my meditation more a part of my life is trying to carry it with me throughout the day. The major religions stress that we are the product of our thoughts. This is a reason why meditation is so important; it yokes our thought more closely with the divine.

This morning I chose the text from Philippians: "The Lord is at hand. Have no anxiety about anything . . . let your requests be made to God. And the peace of God, which passes all understanding, will keep your hearts and your minds in Christ Jesus" (4:5–7). I had been facing a very difficult situation in which anxiety would be a normal human reaction. I believe that under the circumstances God led me to this passage. Briefly, my meditation caused me to realize that if I truly trusted God I would not be anxious. This then led me to think about our tendency not to take the words of Christ at face value. What does this kind of belief consist of? What about trusting God? Is this a gift that comes from him or can we develop it ourselves? Though this is a truncated version of what for me was a highly significant meditation, it might give you a clue to a typical approach.

We live in a noise-polluted world and it is difficult to find periods of silence. Yet it is in silence that we are able to bring ourselves more easily into the presence of God. Because we are not stimulated by sounds and sensations we are far more aware of what is going on within ourselves. Historically, silence has been a way of preparation to reach communion with God.

There is a point where meditation may slide into contemplation, a nonverbal, unstructured relationship with God. You are more consciously in his presence. He floods your whole being with his love, his radiance, his warmth. You *know!* It is not necessarily a better state than meditation and you cannot force it. Leave it to God and follow your meditations. It is, however, another form of orientation toward God.

Prayer

Prayer is one of the simplest, and yet one of the most complex acts to perform. It is simple because it is a direct relationship with God, extending from conversation with him to the silence of just being in his presence. It is complex because of the human tendency to make simple and beautiful things complex. But through prayer we tend to become simpler and more of a whole person rather than various split personalities.

The truth is that we know very little about prayer. The times we run into the most trouble is when we think we are experts. Thomas Merton stressed that:

One cannot begin to face the real difficulties of the life of prayer and meditation unless one is first perfectly content to be a beginner and really experience for himself as one who knows little or nothing and has a desperate need to learn the bare rudiments. Those who think they "know" from the beginning will never in fact come to know anything. We do not want to be beginners. But let us be convinced of the fact that we will never be anything else but beginners all our life.*

A tremendous amount of material has been written about prayer. Formulas have been devised, particular routines established. But none of this is really important.

It is best to remember simply that God is our loving Father. We are consulting him, laying the needs of ourselves and of others before him so that he may supply them as his loving wisdom directs. God knows our wants. It is we who are not always sure. Prayer is putting ourselves into a right relationship with God so that his desires for us become our desires. This is so much easier said than done. It takes practice and persistence. It is work!

Our whole tendency is toward an impatient anxiety. We're convinced that we know exactly what is best for us. Even Christ faced this problem, for while he was waiting for Judas to betray him he asked God to spare him from the coming ordeal. Yet he knew that God had a purpose for him, and he added the words we find so hard to say: "But your will be done." Not my will, God, but yours.

How difficult it is to take this step of truly meaning "your will be done." We fear that God is going to have some dreadful experience in store for us. Indeed, there may be a time when he will have a special task for us to do. And if he does, it is he who will supply us with the strength and the means to do it. But somehow we always expect the worst, forgetting that Jesus said: "I came that they may have life, and have it abundantly" (John 10:10).

God wants us to be healthy, not impoverished physically, mentally,

Contemplation (New York: Image Books, 1971).

or spiritually. He wants us to be fully developed personalities, the best of ourselves. The trouble is that we do not really believe this. We agree that Jesus was a sensationally fine man. We would *like* to believe in the reality of God, and it would be a wonderful thing if we could really convince ourselves that Jesus was the Son of God. But somehow to our logical minds it does not make sense.

We will never satisfy ourselves if we try to work it out logically, because we are attempting to describe God in human terms and all we are doing is looking into a mirror of ourselves. At some point we have to take that "leap of faith" that Kierkegaard urges. You will find then that God *is* real. The presence of Jesus in your life will become more of an actuality.

Perhaps what is most important is that over a period of time prayer brings a change in one's approach to life. We begin to look at the world through the eyes of Jesus. We cannot see objects and relationships as clearly as he, but we begin to achieve an understanding of the nature of truth. Peace throughout the world and the alleviation of suffering is not going to be brought about by rhetoric, charisma, or emotion, but rather by intelligent, loving, God-inspired activity.

So few ever consciously practice the presence of God in their lives. Yet this can be done effectively through prayer. The heart of Christianity lies in prayer, but today many in the Church have put their main stress on activity, forgetting that their true strength and relevance is always rooted in prayer. The Church's activity in the world is God-directed, and this direction is shaped by prayer.

Many people think they have to be uncomfortable to pray properly. This is not true. As in meditation, it is best not to be aware of your body. Traditionally, standing or kneeling has been an act of reverence and obedience. However, one may pray equally well sitting or lying down.

If there is any one thing to emphasize about prayer it is to keep it *simple,* keep it honest, keep it from rambling. We can fool ourselves and other people, but not God. And never ask in prayer for any blessing until you are sure your mind is turned to Jesus Christ, for he is the one who ushers you into the divine presence.

It is difficult to try to classify prayer precisely, for one form tends to overlap another. There are, however, certain broad catagories that are useful to know.

Vocal prayer is not necessarily using one's voice. The expression implies the use of a set form of words often said silently, such as the Lord's Prayer. Or it may be prayer from any formal service of worship.

Mental prayer, in contrast, is that prayer in which we do not use words at all, or if we do they are spontaneous, giving expression to our own thoughts. It is known also as the Prayer of Attention, for it is a holding of one's attention on God. Meditation is a form of mental prayer.

As Truman Dicken suggests in *The Crucible of Love:* "the practical difference between vocal and mental prayer is reduced to a very simple question: do you find that you need set forms of words in order to pray, or do you not?"*

Both types of prayers may include *intercessions;* that is, prayers for the needs of others. We can include *petitions* for our own needs as well.

Mental prayer gives many people difficulty, as it should, for prayer is a creative act and the most important of our religious activities. What we are after is to develop contant awareness of living in the presence of God. According to Dicken, St. Theresa of Avila, one of the great Western mystics, stressed that:

Though we cannot all learn mental prayer, we can all love, and it is our love which is the measure of our real progress. The basic rules for prayer are thus identical whatever our procedure: our progress depends upon our love and our constant habit of prayer, our practice of Christian virtues and our humility and detachment. At the same time, it is our prayer which makes it possible for God to increase in us these virtues. Prayer is the doorway by which God gives us his intimate grace.

Prayers of grace form the third grouping. Little will be said about them, for this is the type of praying that is out of our hands. They are truly an *immediate* contact with God. This is not a type of prayer we can acquire ourselves, for it is given to us. It is supernatural prayer. As you read further in some of the spiritual classics, you will learn more about this form of praying.

At the end of your prayers always remember to thank God for

*New York: Sheed & Ward, 1963.

having solved the problems you have given him, remembering Jesus' promise: "Again I say to you, if two of you agree on earth about anything they ask, it will be done for them by my Father in heaven. For where two or three are gathered in my name, there am I in the midst of them" (Matt. 18:19–20).

Jesus gave the world a new principle of prayer, prayer that is offered and granted *in my name.* Prayer *in the name of Christ* means that we pray as his representatives, as he would pray in our place.

Use "flash" prayers throughtout the day. These are mini-prayers to help keep your "cool," to calm someone, to comfort a stranger who looks unhappy, for courage, and so on.

A type of praying that has given me tremendous support and that should be classified under *vocal prayer* is known as the "Jesus prayer." It apparently came out of the East and has been known since the early years of Christianity. There are variations, but essentially it goes: "Lord Jesus Christ, have mercy on me." Its effect lies in that you are acknowledging Jesus and not only asking forgiveness, but asking for the strength to do his will. This prayer is repeated frequently throughout the day, literally hundreds of times. The words should not be said by rote; you should think about them. It is your awareness of the words that brings you consciously into God's presence, fulfilling Jesus' injunction to "pray without ceasing."

St. Francis of Assisi used the phrase: "My God and my all." This appeals to me more, for it is easier to say and can be used in an exuberantly joyous sense as well as for penitence. It seems to express the completeness of God. He is not only my God in a personal sense, but he is also absolutely everything to me.

Many people use another variation of these forms, repeating only the word God, or Jesus, or Lord Jesus Christ. We can attach other prayers to these words. They are tied to them like the string at the end of a kite and lifted to God. For example, "My God and my all, help me not to be anxious while I am waiting for the decision." These prayer phrases may be used in meditation, repeating the words slowly again and again, letting them absorb us completely.

There is a problem you should know about. Though you may start using short prayers throughout the day with great enthusiasm, you will find invariably that after a few days you realize suddenly that somehow this form of praying has slipped away from you. Try to persist and pick up where you have left off. As you improve you will find them a real aid in spiritual growth.

Speaking in Tongues

Here we can give this subject only the briefest mention. Chapter 15 lists a book under "Prayer" that treats tongues fully. Speaking in tongues is another form of prayer and is one of the manifestations of the Holy Spirit. It is one of the charismatic graces. Charisma is a spiritual gift or talent. In Christianity it is exemplified by the power of healing, speaking in tongues, interpreting tongues or prophesying. Today a number of Christians are involved in these through what is known as the Charismatic Movement. The authority for speaking in tongues comes through the Holy Spirit during Pentecost as described in Acts: "They were all filled with the Holy Spirit and began to speak in other tongues" (2:4).

Speaking in tongues is a communication between you and God in what appears to be a supernatural language that only your soul and God can understand. It is beyond your own mental comprehension. It is a prayer inspired by the Holy Spirit. "For one who speaks in a tongue speaks not to men but to God" (1 Cor. 14:2). Aloud it may sound like any unknown, rapidly spoken foreign language. It has nothing to do with wild rantings or shouting. The way to do it is to begin moving your lips and vocal cords, either aloud or to yourself, asking God to help you. Though Paul spoke in tongues frequently, he emphasized that generally one should do this silently since it is for one's own benefit rather than for others (see 1 Cor. 14:4, 19).

The reason one speaks in tongues is that God knows our needs and problems better than we. And so when we are puzzled it is best to rely on the Holy Spirit to pray for us.

Self-Examination and Reflection

Just prior to going to sleep it is important to take a minute or two to review your whole day, trying to recall if there was anything you did or said that you believe was wrong, and then to ask God's pardon. *The Book of Common Prayer* speaks to this need. Its prayer is a magnificent approach. In giving it here I have substituted "I" for "we."

> Most Merciful God
> I confess that I have sinned against you
> in thought, word and deed:
> I have not loved you with my whole heart.
> I have not loved my neighbor as myself.
> I pray you of your mercy
>   forgive what I have been,
>   amend what I am,
>   direct what I shall be,
> that I may delight in your will,
> and walk in your ways,
> through Jesus Christ our Lord.

In the presence of God we think of the events of the day and see other possibilities. This is the time to compare what actually did happen and to measure these events against our Christian standards.

When I criticized John, was it gossip to build my own ego or was it because I was trying to give a sincere evaluation? Could I have said what I did in a more constructive and helpful way? I lost my temper. Could I have avoided it, not by repressing my anger, but by some other action that would have circumvented the confrontation that brought it on? I didn't like that girl. I thought, how stupid she looks. She thinks she's so cool, but no one else does. But am I being jealous? Or is it my own insecurity? Could I have helped her in some way? Was I building up a wall of hate between us? Maybe she's really unhappy.

One can become morbidly introspective as one sifts through the day. But that's not the point. It is to try to see how by putting Christian love to work consistently we can avoid hurting others and ultimately ourselves.

The writer-director Elia Kazan said in a radio interview: "We have to put all our sins on a table so we can see them. Otherwise we'll kid ourselves and say we don't have any." The French priest Michel Quoist pretends that God is replying to someone asking forgiveness:

> Ask my pardon
> And get up quickly.
> You see it's not falling that is the worst,
> But staying on the ground.*

Church

Attend church regularly. You need to witness as part of a fellowship and to grow with it, to be with like-minded people. It is through the community of faith that we participate on a wider basis. It is by sharing our joy and our concerns with those who really care that we are comforted and strengthened.

A layman told me that at Sunday worship, or while sitting in the quiet of an empty church during the week, solutions to troubling problems came to her.

Partake of Holy Communion frequently, for the words "Do this in remembrance of me" are more than mere links in an old tradition. They embody the very spirit of Christ.

Though you need the Church, it also needs you. It needs you more than as a worshiper. It needs to have you as an integral part of its activities. For *you are the Church.* It is not only a building with stained glass windows and beautiful organ music. The Church is the body of Christ and you are part of it.

The concept of community as it involves the Church is fully developed in Chapter 8.

You can be certain that at some point you will encounter what are known as "dry" periods, when prayer seems to require tremendous effort, when God seems to be in another galaxy, when you feel empty of any spiritual feelings. The technical name for this state is *acedia.*

One answer is that you may have been haphazard in following your way of life, such as daily prayer, and the like. It will always happen and you will begin to slip back down the slopes you have been climbing.

On the other hand, if you have been seriously working at increasing your faith even though the going has been tough, you can be sure it

Prayers (New York: Sheed & Ward, 1963).

is God's own way of strengthening you. In a sense it is analogous to Paul's advice to the Corinthians: "I fed you with milk, not solid food; for you were not ready for it" (1 Cor. 3:2). God is now giving you solid food. He is testing your spiritual muscles. If you can, talk to your minister, or find someone else who is experienced in the life of the spirit who can help you through this period. Above all persist in your way of life. You will soon be scaling new spiritual heights. "I have the strength to face all conditions by the power that Christ gives me" (Phil. 4:13, *Good News for Modern Man*).

CHAPTER TWELVE

Why Sacraments?

The new life *in Christ* is life in communion with him and his people. Along with our worship, it is in spirit and in truth. Although it is spirit it is *in* us, in the world, in space and time. It is sacramental.

A lot of misunderstanding exists about the meaning of sacrament. In the minds of some people it is often connected with magic and its "mumbo-jumbo." That is the last thing it is. It is something that is visible, yet tells us about the invisible. It is secular as water, bread, and wine are secular, yet these secular things are holy in the sacraments.

The dominical sacraments (of or pertaining to Christ) are those of Baptism and Holy Communion. They were authorized by our Lord. We understand them as the visible signs of invisible grace. Some branches of the church include confirmation, penance, extreme unction, marriage, and ecclesiastical orders. These may be defined as ecclesiastical sacraments, which are believed to transmit grace to the souls of the recipients.

Sacrament means the action of God by which common things are consecrated and made holy. With the eyes of faith we see the sacraments as the sign and pledge of God's covenant with us. In Roman times a soldier bound himself to the emperor by an oath, or *Sacramentum.* It signified a sacred act. In the letters of Pliny the Younger to the Emperor Trajan (c. A.D. 112) he mentions that Christians at worship bound themselves by a sacrament (or oath) to Christ as God.

As Christians today we do the same. The consequence is that the loyalty we give completely to our Lord influences all of our other loyalties. We are citizens of two kingdoms. A Scottish reformer visited King James VI in his Scottish palace at Falkland before he became King of England. In an argument that ensued, the reformer said, "I would remind you, your majesty, that there are two kingdoms, and two Kings in Scotland. You are King of one, but Christ is King of the other, and of that Kingdom, you Sire, are but the humblest member."

Wherever we live, we live for Christ; we are bound to him by our *Sacramentum.* And to this sacred oath the sacraments are witnesses.

Baptism

Baptism is by water and the spirit. The water alone is insufficient. It is symbolic of our cleansing from the sins of our old life when our loyalty was to the world. It is also the recognition that our new life is lived within the actual community of Christ's people.

There are those who practice the ceremony of immersion to illustrate these points. And there are those who sprinkle, or pour, water on the babies of Christian families in the belief that the faith of the believing family will bring each child into the new covenant God has made with his people through the atoning work of Jesus Christ. The effective work of this sacrament is not because of any magical virtue in the water or the administrant. It is in the love of Christ and in the activity of the Holy Spirit. The believer, who confesses with his heart and lips that Jesus is his or her Lord, is in the spirit.

Those who have been received into Christ's Church at infancy confirm the baptismal vows made in their behalf when they come to the years of conscious choice and commitment. There is a growing consensus of opinion, however, that baptism, in this overtly secular age, should be reserved for adults. This would affirm that we receive our new life from Christ and not from society. But above all, as Christians, we must see the sacrament of baptism in the same light as Paul did when he wrote: "By baptism we were buried with him, and lay dead, in order that, as Christ was raised from the dead in the splendor of the Father, so also we might set our feet upon the new path of life" (Rom. 6:4, NEB).

The Lord's Supper

As Christians we gather round our Lord's table. From him we receive the nourishment we need for our spiritual growth and development. His words are very important to use in this matter:

"I tell you this: the truth is, not that Moses gave you the bread from heaven, but that my Father gives you the real bread from heaven. The bread that God gives comes down from heaven and brings life to the world." They said to him, "Sir, give us this bread now and always." Jesus said to them, "I am the bread of life. Whoever comes to me shall never be hungry, and whoever believes in me shall never be thirsty" (John 6:32–35, NEB).

The service of the Lord's Supper, Holy Communion, or Eucharist, is built around these words of Jesus at the Last Supper:

> And he took bread,
>   gave thanks,
>   and broke it;
>   and he gave it to them,
> with the words: "This is my body" (Luke 22:19, NEB).

He Took Bread

is the offertory. We present the bread and wine of everyday existence to be transformed by the action of Christ in our midst into a meal of communion with him and his brethren.

In the early days of the Church everyone brought something—wine, bread, water, money. These were presented by the congregation at the Holy Table to be set apart for the service of God. As in the feeding of the 4,000 and the 5,000, the surplus from the feast was used to feed, clothe, and house the needy.

Along with these gifts, each worshiper presents himself "to be a reasonable, holy, and living sacrifice." God takes these bruised and broken lives of ours. He heals them, renews them, makes them holy, and gives them back to us for his service in the world.

Gave Thanks

In a contemporary Jewish home, for example, the head of the household might say, as he passes the wine and the bread: "Praised be Thou, O Lord our God, King of the universe, who hast created the fruit of the vine. Praised be Thou, O Lord our God, King of the universe, who causest the earth to yield for all." The prayer of Jesus was probably similar.

When we consider the setting of the Last Supper—Jesus' betrayal by Judas Iscariot and his imminent death at the hands of the Roman soldiers—we have a better understanding of what giving thanks means. In hardship or suffering we are more inclined to blame God than to praise him. When we thank him for providing for our every need, we tend to forget that the provision he has made for our salvation has been made through the sacrifice of his beloved Son.

When Abraham was about to kill his son on a mountaintop God stopped him. For a sacrifice, he provided instead a ram caught in a thorny bush. John the Baptist understood the costly nature of our Lord's love when he said of Jesus: "Look, there is the Lamb of God; it is he who takes away the sin of the world" (John 1:29, NEB).

And Broke It

The broken bread is what St. Augustine termed "the visible sign of an invisible grace." We get a grip, through this action, on the reality of Christ's sacrifice. His suffering and death were no illusion. He was nailed to a cross; his body was pierced by a sword or lance; he died. He died for me, for you. "This is my body."

And He Gave It To Them

This act of giving makes possible our communion, or being in fellowship with him. Paul rightly speaks of this mystery in these words: "When we bless 'the cup of blessing,' is it not a means of sharing in the blood of Christ? When we break the bread, is it not a means of sharing in the body of Christ? Because there is one loaf, we, many as we are, are one body; for it is one loaf of which we all partake" (1 Cor. 10:16–17, NEB). In the act of communion, therefore, we have the assurance, the comfort, the knowledge, that our Lord is with us now and to the end of time.

The sacrament of the Lord's Supper is a commemoration of our Lord's sacrifice. By our obedience in remembering (see Luke 22:19; 1 Cor. 11:24) we become one with the disciples who were there in the Upper Room when Jesus said: "This is my body." We are also one with them when they said to our risen Savior: "My Lord, and my God."

As well as being a sacrament of remembrance it is a sacrament of declaration. All that may be said in words about the revelation of God in his Son Jesus, our Lord, is never enough. Its meaning transcends description. What cannot be said is declared in action: "For every time you eat this bread and drink the cup, you proclaim the death of the Lord, until he comes" (1 Cor. 11:26 NEB).

Christ is truly present with us in saving power. To this the sacraments testify.

As a prisoner of war of the Japanese I learned the deep meaning of the Lord's Supper. Along with others, I was forced to work seven days a week as a slave. There were no sacramental days and feasts to redeem our wasted time or to give us hope until by the action of the Holy Spirit a fellowship was created to honor Christ. The ugly prison camp of suffering men became holy and our suffering was transcended. Christ's love reached out through us to our enemies. Our prison became a community of liberated men.

On the Easter morning of 1945 a large number of us met secretly before dawn to celebrate the resurrection of our living liberator, secretly because services of worship were forbidden. As we shared the broken body of our Lord—small rolls made of rice—and drank the blood of the New Covenant—fermented rice water—the sun rose in sacramental splendor. We who worshiped were one in the moment of sacrament with God and his creation, with the Church in heaven and on earth, with all men whom our Lord's sacrifice had made neighbors.

The Sacramental Life

The best answer to the question: "How should I live in the world?" is to be found in our Lord's great prayer of love in John 17.

Although our life has become different from the only one the world may give us, we are not commanded to flee from the world. Instead, we are to live in it. As God has sent his Son into the world, so does Christ send his disciples. We are set apart by the consecration of the truth in Christ. Our given vocation is to be his agents and mediators of the divine joy.

Jesus' prayer was for his disciples *then*. It is also for his disciples *now*. "But it is not for these alone that I pray, but for those also who through their words put their faith in me." This expresses the succession of faith that stretches from Palestine to America, from A.D. 30 to the 1970s. "*Their* words" refers to those who live and speak in the power of their faith and thereby form a sacramental bridge between the first and the later disciples.

The Christian Year

Our everyday lives are ordered by the calendar year, the school year, and the succession of national holidays. But, as Christians, we should be aware of the Christian year. To understand the sacraments, their richness and particular meaning for us, we need to know the magnificent and beautiful cycle of seasons that make up the Christian year

Advent: This is the season to prepare for Christmas. It begins on the fourth Sunday before Christmas, ending at midnight Christmas Eve. It is a time of expectancy, reminding us of the thousands of years before the coming of Christ when the world was waiting for its Savior.

Christmas: It is the Feast of the Nativity, celebrating the birth of God in the world and the birth of Jesus the man. It is the day of potential spiritual birth for all people.

Epiphany: This season after Christmas celebrates God's showing himself forth in Jesus Christ as Savior and Redeemer of the world. It begins in January on Epiphany Day, which commemorates the visit of the Magi to the infant Jesus.

Lent: Beginning with Ash Wednesday and including the forty weekdays before Easter, Lent remembers the forty-day fast of Jesus. It is a time of reflection and penance. Some give up what they think are harmful habits and also little pleasures, while others try to do acts of charity for others. This is a good time to read more about the things of the spirit. Our awareness of Christ's mission of salvation is heightened in Lent.

Easter: This is the time of the supreme miracle, of Christ's resurrection. The words that are said in some churches when the Paschal Candle is lit reflect the glory of this moment: "May the light of Christ, in glory rising again, dispel the darkness of heart and mind."

From Pentecost to Advent: "This long section of the year uses the story of Christ's public life and the writings of the Apostles to teach us the truth of our faith. The time after Pentecost is the first chance to use our new power to be witnesses."*

Within the seasons there are special days given to the various saints who reached out to the world, sharing God's love. A good liturgical calendar that lists these special days in an inexpensive and interesting investment. Stores selling religious items will have them.

*Ethel Marbach, *Family Liturgical Customs* (St. Meinrad, Ind.: Abbey Press).

CHAPTER THIRTEEN

Witnessing

Webster's dictionary defines *witness* as "to make known to others (by speech or conduct) the religious experience one has undergone or the religious truths in which one believes."

Many of us are shy and may find it difficult to go to a stranger and initiate a conversation. Yet, it is a natural reaction to tell people about an experience that has deep meaning for us. Think what happens when someone encounters the reality and power of Jesus Christ in his life. It is such an explosively joyous and overwhelming feeling that he has an irresistable urge to rush out and tell the world about it.

A college girl said: "My first impulse was to tell others and I know I was loud about it. I wanted to tell everyone. It's so great you want to share the joy. Then after a while you calm down and you know when and where to witness and to share."

Is there a *where* and a *when* to witness? Many people have ambivalent feelings about this. Some believe you must try to reach everyone regardless of place and time. Others think that such an approach can be offensive.

Billy Graham's mass crusades have always been a center of controversy. Yet I have known people who have had their interest awakened and have gone on to conversion. They might have been reached in other ways but they were not. We live in a world that is mostly pagan and the sincere electronic-age evangelist can open the door for the Holy Spirit. When a crusade is televised at least for one hour people are given an alternative to the usual nightly fare.

The story of black evangelist Tom Skinner is well known. The son of a minister in New York's Harlem, he rejected religion and was very much a part of the local gangs. One day he listened to a radio evangelist and became irritated because the man spoke so poorly. But that day God touched young Skinner. It was a turning point and the beginning of conversion.

Witnessing in all forms has obviously been effective. In 1800 only 5 percent of the population belonged to a church. By 1900 the number had grown to 36 percent, and in 1955 it soared to 60 percent. Today the figure is closer to 40 percent.*

What we should remember about witnessing is that we are not all enjoined to stop people on the street or to testify before an audience. Nor are the techniques of the mass media necessarily the best approach. Witnessing takes many forms. As a minister aptly stated, so often only the aggressive people get the credit. This is not meant to decry such an approach, but only to say that the aggressive, bold or enterprising witness is only one method.

We will witness best if we remain true to the type of person we are. If you are quiet and retiring there is no need to feel guilty about your reluctance to speak out in public. If you are more of an extrovert do not feel bad if some people criticize your approach. If your heart is open to the Holy Spirit, what you do will be right.

Some people object to the words "saved" and "witnessed." They may seem to be trite, or to belong to another age. But we should remember that the impact of a word is not the same for every person. One's understanding and response to a word goes deeper than its dictionary meaning, because his total, individual association is also involved with the word. Did he first come across it under pleasant circumstances? Does the word relate to an unhappy incident in his life? Perhaps it has something to do with his life attitude. Clever writers like George Bernard Shaw in *Major Barbara* or Frank Loesser in *Guys and Dolls* have lampooned organizations such as The Salvation Army and the words they use. Because of this we may tend to be somewhat sensitive and supercilious about them.

We don't look down on *save* when a life guard *saves* a drowning

---

*Paulus Scharpff, *History of Evangelism* (Grand Rapids, Mich.: William B. Eerdmans, 1966).

person, or a fireman *saves* a child from a burning home, or when Helmer cries out in Ibsen's *The Doll's House:* "Yes it is true! I am saved! Nora, I am saved!"

What a strong word *saved* is in a religious sense, for we are saved from all that which causes misery in the world and are brought into a new way of life. Only someone who has experienced this can understand fully what the word "saved" means.

In *History of Evangelism*—evangelism being an effort to spread the Gospel—Scharpff delineates the area of witnessing:

The evangelistic message is a persistent, pleading invitation to seize the proffered hour for repentance from sin and for surrender to Christ. It emphasizes the *now* and *today*—the primary purpose of the evangelistic message is not general Christian instruction in and improvement of the moral life; its first concern, rather, is to awaken souls from spiritual death, to bring them rebirth by the power of the Holy Spirit.

Actually, the trend today in evangelism is to teach the new Christian how to grow in practicing God's love in everyday life. To be saved is just the first step. Christ lives in us, but it is through our efforts that we live in Christ.

When one reads the history of the Church and the lives of dedicated souls, one cannot help but be in awe of their commitment, their love, their achievements. It is too bad that many of their individual names are swallowed up in history and we do not know much about them.

There is a biblical authority for witnessing. Jesus calls us today in the same way he called out to Simon and Andrew as they were fishing: "Follow me and I will make you become fishers of men" (Mark 1:17). Among the last words that our Lord spoke to the eleven assembled disciples were: "Go therefore and make disciples of all nations, baptizing them in the name of the Father and of the Son and of the Holy Spirit, teaching them to observe all that I have commanded you" (Matt. 28:19–20).

Jesus very clearly expected his teachings to be spread throughout the world. On the face of it, what an impossible task that must have seemed for eleven humble, unknown men in a remote part of the world. Yet, as one minister said who had taken over an unpromising church: "My first service bred my first conversion. That's how you start—with one, then two, then more, and yet more."

Paul in his second letter to the Corinthians writes: "So we are ambassadors for Christ, God making his appeal through us" (5:20). Paul roamed the Mediterranean area, often putting his life on the line for his beliefs. He was stoned, whipped, shipwrecked, imprisoned. But due to his witnessing we have a Christian Church, for it was he who in town after town planted the seed of Christ in a few hearts. Through them, others were converted.

There are people who are Christlike and concern themselves with those who desperately need God's help.

Arthur Blessitt is one of them. He is an amazing man who has a place of refuge on Sunset Strip in Los Angeles called His Place, His referring to Jesus. This combination church–night club has performed a dynamic and unique ministry to thousands of young people who have lost their way in life, who are messed up with dope, drugs, alcohol, and sex. He has also established Halfway House, which provides a transition spot where one can firm up a bit more in the faith before returning to face the world.

Blessitt has no compunction about telling people what Christ can do for them whether it is in a law court or on a street corner. He says: "I consider street-witnessing as important to our ministry as His Place and Halfway House. The timorous, the troubled, the suspicious could often be reached in no other way. Some of the most gloriously saved Christians I know had their first interest in Christ generated in a sidewalk contact. The Lord doesn't mind where a soul is won."*

W. A. Haberern, an insurance agent, consistently witnesses in his own quiet way. An important element in his witnessing is his church, which is extremely active in helping new Christians grow into their faith. During a rainstorm he took shelter under a storefront awning. A young man and a girl scurried in beside him. There was something about the couple that touched my friend. Their blue jeans were old, the rest of their clothing in poor shape. They themselves looked tired and unhealthy.

He introduced himself and after a bit invited them to a Bible study class. They said they would come, but of course did not. Several days

*Arthur Blessitt, with Walter Wagner, *Turned on to Jesus* (New York: Hawthorn Books, 1971).

later he saw them on the street, and again quietly suggested they would be welcome. They did not appear. A third time he met them by chance and once more invited them. This time they came and from that moment on their life-style began to change.

Rick and Jenny had lived a sordid life. Utterly without money, Rick sold his wife to another man so they could have a place to stay. Drugs took whatever money they had left over. They were on welfare and were emotionally and physically sick. At the age of eighteen, Jenny had lost most of her teeth. The welfare department gave them up and said they were hopeless. Undoubtedly they would be on welfare the rest of their lives.

But bureaucracy did not reckon with the power of Christ. Both Jenny and Rick were converted. To the amazement of everyone except the church, Rick located a good job and is holding on to it. Instead of their old hovel, they now have a pleasant apartment. Both of them are witnessing to others, bringing their friends to church. It took almost six months to achieve this, but what would have happened had Haberern been reluctant to speak to them or given up when they did not come the first time?

How do you approach someone you have never met before? You will be most at ease and convincing when you say whatever seems to come naturally, to speak the truth from your heart. We can speak with confidence because we know how we have been changed: our personal relationships are changed, our conception of work and duty and pleasure are changed, our relationship to God is changed. Our lives have been redirected, re-created, remade. We have joy.

Sometimes the strongest witness is by example.

Neil Lebhar, a college student, said that a few years ago he and some others had formed a Christian commune in Martha's Vineyard, a summer resort. "When people came into the house and saw us working together—cooking, sweeping, caring for each other, loving one another—this was witnessing without the frills. They could understand and see what Christianity is all about. When he lived, everyone could see how much Paul loved people. We tried to show the same thing."

This witness was in sharp contrast to the quality of life most of us encounter. It could not help but appeal to a sensitive person and make him want to know more. It is a fulfillment of what Jesus has asked of us: "A new commandment I give to you, that you love one another; even as I have loved you" (John 13:34).

It is the Gospel that counts and it is the Holy Spirit that will convert.

Sometimes you will feel guilty because you have not brought about a particular conversion. But conversion is God's business. Our business is to present the Good News, to be faithful. We work with God, not without him. If we take conversion as our responsibility, we are mistaken, for then we are taking on the sovereignty of God.

Witness where you can, the way you feel is right for you. And before you do, you might repeat one or both of the following prayers:

"Dear Jesus, give me strength and guidance for this witness in your name."

"O God, glorify yourself today at my expense. Send the bill—anything, Lord. I set no price. I will not dicker or bargain. Glorify yourself. I'll take the consequences."

Books are another aspect of the mass audience witness, and some authors such as C. S. Lewis have been read by millions. A book is especially useful for it can be marked up and reread. One can think deeply about a passage, extracting the full import of it. Books can change lives.

Laurance, a friend of mine in California, had been heavily into drugs. He was in jail a number of times for robbery and assault. When out on bail one last time he was in San Francisco with no friends, no money, no where to go. The Salvation Army was the only place he could think of, and he was welcomed there. As he sat in a recreation room he pulled out a book on religion to fill the time. To Laurance, God was like one of the unknown stars in space. Possibly he existed, but if so he was remote.

Then a certain passage caught him: "God is love." That was all. *God is love.* But it was enough. For some reason it pulled everything together for Laurance. God is love. God is real. God is a living force. He realized this living force was in Christ.

He completely changed his ways and became a new man, joining a church, marrying and raising a family, working at a responsible job. He is one of the gentlest and most generous men I know. He became such a different person that he legally changed his name to Newman. "Therefore, if any one is in Christ, he is a new creation; the old has passed away, behold, the new has come" (2 Cor. 5:17).

One of Ernest Gordon's first churches in this country was a small one in the distant suburbs. In the general area there was no outreach through adult education. With the cooperation of several other churches, a combined meeting was held for study. The first hour was spent on the New Testament, the second on church history. He discovered that the people knew little about either. How could someone be mature in the faith when he had no idea of what it was all about. Gradually a new spirit entered the churches as people began to understand and to grow. The discipline of study is a highly important aspect of evangelism.

The Gospel is the foundation stone. It was there before you or me, before the sacraments, before the Church. The Gospel is the most important way that the Holy Spirit speaks to us. It is the witness of Jesus to the world. It is the authority of Jesus. The most logical place for the Gospel to be preached is in church as a continuing witness, a continuing community of faith.

"We are probably wrong to spend so much effort looking for ways of communication. We should be looking for *men* who communicate. They might be few and hard to find, yet the Church depends on them."*

Preaching is vital in communicating the Word, for we need to be continually witnessed to as well as to witness, for we cannot give what we do not have. Once, when listening to the words from John 10:16, the realization struck me as it never had before that only in Christ can we truly be brothers and sisters: "And I have other sheep, that are not of this fold; I must bring them also, and they will heed my voice. So there shall be one flock, one shepherd." I can be a close friend with a Buddhist, or a Taoist, or someone of another faith. But never can I be his brother except through Jesus Christ. It is only through him that the whole world will be united in peace and love.

A missionary once told a tribe of American Indians of the love that God the Father had for them through Jesus. To the Indians it was like a new revelation. An old chief said: "When you spoke of the great spirit just now did I hear you say, 'our Father'?"

*Ernest Gordon, "Communicating the Gospel," in *The Church in the Modern World,* ed. George Johnston and Wolfgang Roth (Toronto: The Ryerson Press, 1967).

"Yes," replied the missionary.

"That is very new and sweet to me," said the chief. "We never thought of the great Spirit as Father. We heard him in the thunder; we saw him in the lightning, the tempest and the blizzard, and we were afraid. So when you tell us that the great Spirit is *our Father* that is very beautiful to us."

The old man paused, and then went on, as he glimpsed the glory of the idea. "Missionary, did you say that the great Spirit is *your* Father?"

"Yes."

"And," said the chief, "did you say that he is *the Indians'* Father?"

"I did."

"Then," said the old chief, like a man upon whom a dawn of joy had burst, "*you and I are brothers.*"

CHAPTER FOURTEEN

The Meaning of Faith

As new Christians we live by faith. This seems reasonable enough until someone asks us what we mean. We aren't sure. Although faith is obvious it is hard to explain. We have also heard so many things said about it that we are confused. We may even have had someone make fun of us as though faith and stupidity were the same thing. They aren't.

Everybody lives by faith of some kind. Without it life would not only be intolerable, but impossible. In its most basic form faith is experienced as conviction, certitude, a mental attitude, insight, a kind of knowledge or loyalty. There is plenty of evidence to show that human beings have an extraordinary capacity for giving their loyalty to all kinds of institutions and causes, most of which are unworthy.

You may think of many examples of misplaced faith that have had disastrous results. Men have believed so strongly in certain causes—Nazism for example—that millions of people have been massacred in consequence. Men have believed so sincerely in money and profits that they have enslaved other human beings. Our daily newspapers and television shows give countless examples of faith gone wrong.

Each of us has faith! What matters supremely is the object of our faith, its fulfillment, and its quality.

What Faith Is Not

It Is Not Wishful Thinking

A school of people has developed who teach that it is wishful thinking. All you have to do is believe that everything will be all right and it will be. If you are traveling by plane, wish as strongly as you can that you will arrive at your destination safely, and you will. If you are looking for a parking place, one will suddenly appear if you take time to wish for it. By inference, those who are involved in trouble or who have crashed in an airplane or failed to find a parking place are lacking in faith.

The Bible never describes faith as wishful thinking. The heroes of faith didn't have an easy time. The prophets were men of vision, the insight of faith, yet over 90 percent of them were executed or exiled. And what about Jesus? In him faith was perfect. He was crucified. His way to the resurrection was through the cross.

Faith as wishful thinking is faith in faith rather than faith in the living God. Those who advocate worshiping success are of this school. They forget that Christianity is a faith for failures. It is God who overcomes our failures, even that of death. Whatever faith is, in the Christian sense, it is never autosuggestion.

It Is Not Magic

In the practice of magic its devotees try to manipulate nature by making it obey the ritualistic duplication of its processes. In that way people have been urged to look upon God as a super Santa Claus. By uttering the right incantations he can be persuaded to give the worshiper his heart's desire.

This isn't faith. When the crowds heard of Jesus' miracle they rushed to see him, hoping, perhaps, that he would do some magic for them and provide their hearts' desires: a wealthy husband, a fancy car, and a mansion. He knew what was in their minds and said: "This generation is an evil generation; it seeks a sign."

There are many who look for magic instead of faith. But we don't manipulate God. We obey him.

Faith Does Not Create God

Sometimes we may be tempted to glorify our conversion or religious experience so much that we give the impression of glorifying our faith rather than God.

I once went with a friend to hear a popular evangelist. I hoped he would have a word to say that would help my friend to commit himself to Christ. The evangelist raged against the evils of contemporary youth, then went on to tell us how good he was. He left us with the impression that what counted was having the same faith as his. What that faith was, and was for, we weren't certain.

I was afraid to ask my friend for his opinion. He gave it to me, however: "He was talking about himself all the time. I thought he might have put in a word for Jesus Christ once in a while. If he has faith, it is in himself."

Faith Is Not Belief in a Religious Slogan

We are sometimes encouraged to believe that faith is simply the acceptance of a particular doctrine or creed. Before the Reformation, leaders in the medieval church taught that a fixed system of dogmas was the truth. The intellectual acceptance of them insured the believers of salvation. To question or disagree with these dogmas could result in a person being condemned to burn at the stake as a heretic or atheist. An atheist of that time was someone who did not believe the right thing about God and the church. By present standards, medieval atheists would be judged very religious indeed.

After the Reformation some people did not learn from the experiences of the past and continued to equate faith with belief in certain formulas. It is important, therefore, to distinguish between believing *about* Jesus Christ and believing *in* him. Creeds and dogmas are *about* him. Saving faith is *in* him.

The Bible is the word of God that tells us of the response of believers to God's word revealed in Jesus Christ. It is the record of those who believed in God and his Son. The Reformers made it very clear that while the Bible is our supreme guide of faith and conduct, it has no ultimate authority unless faith is created in the life of the reader by the action of the Holy Spirit. Reluctantly, perhaps, we have to admit that the devil and his colleagues can quote Scripture as fluently as anyone. Jesus, you will recall, accused his opponents of searching the Scripture but refusing to come to him for eternal life.

Faith Is Not Moralism or Legalism

Along with the error of mistaking faith for belief about right doctrines is the danger of thinking that faith can be limited to a series of ethical principles or rational laws. This is a temptation every Christian has to face. It is easier to proclaim a compact list of religious propositions than it is to preach Christ. With him the message is in the messenger.

Many of the agnostics I have counseled have been forced into that position by the harshness of the laws imposed upon them. Their lives were imprisoned in a cell of "don'ts": Don't think for yourself, don't be happy, don't question authority, don't speak unless you are spoken to, don't enjoy the good life God has given, don't do anything in case you sin. According to the "don't" philosophy, a stone or a vegetable is highly moral because it doesn't do all the things that a legalistic code says we shouldn't.

Christ never came to imprison anyone. He came to set us free from the prison cell of don'ts. That's why Paul exclaimed: "For freedom Christ has set us free; stand fast therefore, and do not submit again to a yoke of slavery" (Gal. 5:1).

What Faith Is

Faith Is Divinely Inspired

The advantage of thinking about what faith is not is that we are reminded of what faith is: it is the gift of God. This is what characterizes us as human beings. Without faith life is impossible. The problems of mankind are caused by its lack on the one hand and by misplacing it on the other. It is the good thing that our Father will never withhold from those who ask him. Regardless of which milestone we may have reached in our eternal pilgrimage, all of us must pray with the father of the epileptic boy, whom Jesus healed: "Lord, I believe, help thou mine unbelief."

We are presented with this gift in order that we may respond to God's initiative. He is the one who taps us on the shoulder. When someone does so we usually have enough intelligence to turn around to see who is there. Faith is this kind of intelligence of response.

A student was convinced that all the ills of society could be cured by applying the correct economic formula. One summer he worked with a social service agency among unemployed miners. As he worked among them he realized that there was no formula. There was little point in telling these men with rotting lungs and no hope that everything was going to be all right for someone else in thirty or fifty years time. What mattered for those men, and for himself, was the quality of life and hope they had now. He was gripped by the conviction that there had to be something good enough and big enough to care for men and women as they are, something that did not ignore human injustice, inadequacy, suffering, and death.

He began to see the cross planted at the intersections of life: at the meetingplaces of misery and despair, selfishness and suffering, greed and power. In the midst of our failures, he saw that God had come in holy love to care for his people, to suffer in that caring, and to overcome those principalities and powers that destroy all that is potentially good.

A lovely girl wrote to say that she was weary of the way men tried to buy and use her beauty. She was depressed. As she walked along a street she saw an elderly couple walking with their arms around each other's waist. Then a ray of sunshine filled a street corner with its warm light. She passed an antique store. In the center of the window there was a crucifix. She stopped to look at it. Her heart skipped with an overwhelming sense of delight. She knew that whatever she was, she was Christ's friend.

In those two instances, the people concerned were grasped by God. They were tapped on the shoulder and responded by turning to him.

Faith Is Trust

In responding to God's initiative by turning to him, we find ourselves in a new relationship in which we have eternal life. Trust is the dynamic that enables people to live openly with each other. In Christ we know that God has opened himself to us as our Father. He trusts us to the extent that his Son died for us. When we see this, what else can we do but trust him who has trusted us so much.

Often the question is asked: "Who can I trust? I can't trust my friends. I can't trust my neighbors. I can't trust my parents. I can't trust my government." There is only one answer. God and none other is worthy of our ultimate trust. This answer has already been given by millions of people throughout the ages. The Psalmist sang out his answer: "When my father and my mother forsake me, then the Lord will take me up"(Ps. 27:10).

Such a cry is the basic recognition that in our experiences everyone may fail us except God. Once we learn to trust him we learn from him to trust others more, even those who have proved themselves to be untrustworthy. In this way the circle of our relationships is increased to include our enemies.

We do not trust Christ because of what he will do for us, such as helping us to get ahead, but because by trusting him we know him better. He is, therefore, the only reward we seek. In trust we put our hand into his to follow him wherever he may lead us.

As we have noted earlier, faith is the human response to the divine initiative. In Jesus we see the revelation and the response as one. As the Incarnate Word he lived the life of perfect response in trust and obedience. One of the most moving scenes in the Gospels takes place in the olive grove of Gethsemane after the Last Supper and before his betrayal. With a hymn of thanksgiving on his lips he went out from the Upper Room into the garden of suffering. His heart was heavy with sorrow. Judas was about to betray him, his disciples to flee from him. They were to break their trust in him. He was lonely. That loneliness is recorded in these words: "My soul is very sorrowful, even to death; remain here, and watch with me" (Matt. 26:38). Then he walked away from them, fell on his face and prayed: "My Father, if it be possible, let this cup pass from me; nevertheless, not as I will, but as thou wilt" (Matt. 26:39).

What a powerful picture of the trusting Son in his willingness to complete his mission of reconciling love! In the classical doctrine of the person of Jesus Christ it is affirmed that in him the human and the divine wills were perfectly one. Thus the ultimate revelation and the ultimate expression of trust and obedience were united in the life of Jesus our Lord.

Faith Is Life

This life by faith is big, divinely big. Don't, therefore, let anyone tempt you to cut it down to inadequate size. Our blessed Lord did not come to limit life but to open it to its abundance. The Gospels do not present us with a grey-faced, defeated man, but with the Lord of life. In him was life, and the life was the light of men. Wherever he went he touched others with his beautiful vitality. People who were dropouts perked up when he came along. Defeated men were so invigorated by him that instead of packing up and calling for the undertaker, they had another go at things. Because of him the dead came to life. To believe in him is to come to life. He never took a scrap of a man's manhood or a woman's womanhood away from them. He enriched, ennobled, and fulfilled them.

The measure of the life he gives is seen in its grandeur in the incident with Martha after the death of her brother Lazarus. She was deeply upset, and said that Lazarus would not have died if only Jesus had arrived in time to cure him. Jesus' reply was in these tremendous words: "I am the resurrection and the life; he who believes in me, though he die, yet shall he live, and whoever lives and believes in me shall never die" (John 11:25–26).

This is a clear definition of the new quality of life Jesus confers upon his people. It is the life beyond the control of purely physical laws. It is the life revealed in Jesus at his resurrection. We receive this life here and now by faith. We don't wait for it until death or the last day. Our life with God through Christ is now. When we worship we celebrate this truth in our recognition that the Church in heaven and the Church on earth share the same divine and eternal life.

Faith Is Intensified Consciousness

Our old life is one in which we were ever conscious of the controls of our natural, cultural, and psychological environments. These conrols limited our consciousness to the lower levels of existence. We were aware of our bedroom, our classroom, our office, and the distances between, and that was about all. Our response of faith is different, for it leads us into God's presence. Harriet Beecher Stowe says in her hymn:

> Still, still with thee, when purple morning breaketh,
> When the birds waketh, and the shadows flee;
> Fairer than morning, lovelier than daylight,
> Dawns the sweet consciousness, I am with thee.

In writing these words she is trying to convey something of the joy we experience in being with God, and not against him. The colors of earth and sky are brilliant, beauty is everywhere, people are your friends, former enemies are now neighbors. What is happening is that you are in communion with Christ, and so you are becoming more aware of his hallmark on the world of your experience. You are increasingly aware of what life is all about.

This new consciousness results in a change of personality. I told a friend that he was the most loving person I had ever met. He replied: "That's due to Christ. When I was a young man I was very conscious of power. That's why I went into politics, and as a reward became president of an industrial firm. Then came a day when I faced a situation that was beyond my power to deal with or understand. My wife was killed in an accident. What I had meant nothing anymore. My one hope in the whole world was Christ. I turned from the love of power to him. I loved him. He changed my whole way of looking at things." Paul counsels us to have the "mind" that was also in Christ Jesus, which results in new personalities: persons who love.

When we grow in faith the intensity of our consciousness increases, we become more aware of our heavenly Father's action and more obedient to his word. I have read the biographies of men and women who were faithful to Christ in the Third Reich and in Communist Russia. All of them paid for their faithfulness with their lives. In reading about them I was struck by the heroism of their witness and the power of their Christian consciousness. They were real persons, so real that death could not destroy their consciousness. They were intensely alive, sharers in the power of the resurrection.

Faith Is a New Vision, Insight, and Outlook

In Dickens's *A Christmas Carol,* the miser Scrooge was a mean character with a narrow vision and a limited outlook. When the love of Christmas reached him he saw things differently. He saw men and women that he had never noticed before. He saw smiling faces where once there had only been blackness.

Because of our new consciousness we see things differently. We begin to see them through the eyes of Christ. Our natural selfishness blinds us to the needs and beauty of others. Our prejudices blind us so that we cannot see people as they are. We see a backward person, or a stupid person, or a black person, or an inferior person. That is the blindness of evil. The eyes of faith see them as those whom Christ loved so much that he died for them.

New sight is given by Jesus in John's story of the man who had been born blind. Though suspicious neighbors and opposing authorities were reluctant to acknowledge the change, the man affirmed: "one thing I know, that though I was blind, now I see" (John 9:25). And with his new sight he was able to see what most of those around him who had had natural vision all their lives did not see. In stages he acknowledged Jesus as a prophet, as God's Son, and as Lord.

To believe in Jesus is to see by faith. It is the only way we may understand the unseen and the intangible activity of God.

Faith Is the Source of Action

Sometimes we may have heard arguments about whether one should have faith or do good works. It is a false argument based on the assumption that faith and action may be separated. The argument for works without faith can only end up in moralism and legalism— that is, the belief that behavior alone, without regard to motivation, is all that matters.

We often know what is good, but we often don't do what we know. The problem is: what moves the will? The Christian answer is faith. Jesus made this clear in his Sermon on the Mount. Righteous behavior is the consequence of being made right with God. We do not try to justify ourselves by pointing to all the good deeds we have accomplished—always fewer than we are prepared to admit—but by pointing to Jesus Christ who has justified us.

Faith Is Fulfillment

The salvation he brings to the world is clearly seen as that of healing, renewing, re-creating, and reconciling. These are the activities of the new creation. By faith in Jesus as Lord we pass from death to life. We become sharers in the benefits of his saving work. We also become more like him as we enter more fully into communion with him.

Physically, we reach our peak of development between the ages of nineteen and twenty-three. Thereafter, physiologists tell us, we go downhill slowly until the bodily functions cease with death. To grow in the fellowship of Christ, however, is to grow in the spirit and to find one's citizenship completed in the city of God. As Paul reminded the Roman Christians: "The kingdom of God is not eating and drinking, but justice, peace, and joy, inspired by the Holy Spirit. He, who thus shows himself a servant of Christ, is acceptable to God and approved by men" (Rom. 14:17–18).

Our new life in Christ's new creation gives us the power to work with God and to become more effective as his servants. Potential talents that have been lying dormant are liberated. The early Christians outloved and outthought the pagans. They were conscious of the Holy Spirit working through them. In *Through the Valley of the Kwai,* Ernest Gordon shows how men of faith transformed a prison camp into a community of love. The works of love were shown in the creation of medicines from jungle plants, an orchestra from bamboo and animals' intestines, a university from people seeking the truth, and a variety of creative services from almost nothing.

My Faith

Faith is always particular, which is why we speak of *my faith.* Faith must be a firsthand experience. Those who sing about the old-fashioned religion being good enough for them, because it was good enough for their old daddy and mom, are in danger of forgetting that all of us have to come one by one to Christ and say: "Lord, I believe in you." The truth of the Gospel that is passed on with the tradition of faith must be appropriated by each one of us. Thus in the creed we must say: "We believe in God the Father Almighty," and so on, because the truth comes to us through the mediation of Christ's community of faith in the world. We are aware of "our faith" only when we know that we are never without this community. But "our" must also be "my."

The faith of Andrew, James, John, and Peter is also "my faith." It is an original and unique event in the cosmos. Something has happened. God has grasped me. I have heard his word. I have come into communion with the Christ to whom his apostles witness in every age. I say "my faith" because I have said "my Lord" to Christ in wondering love.

My faith is the moment of second birth. It is the moment when I know with certitude that the Father's love, the Son's death, and the Holy Spirit's power is for me. With the one-time blind man, I can say: "I was blind, now I see."

We are liberated and justified by the faith God has created in us. This is not of my doing. It is the action of God within me.

The man Jesus whom the apostles heard, saw, and touched is my Lord, here and now. I know him in the power of his resurrection. The Christ who is God's deed and word is with me, and for me. He has sought me out, and found me. I am therefore filled with wonder and delight. Paul tells us: "Examine yourselves, to see whether you are holding to your faith. Test yourselves. Do you not realize that Jesus Christ is in you?" (2 Cor. 13:5). Therefore my faith is in Christ and by faith he shares his life with me.

It is through Jesus we understand what faith is all about. In him we see faith working, facing the challenges of life, praying to our Father, and obeying his will. He shows us the Father as the object of our faith. We believe in Christ. In believing, we know him to be the way, the truth, and the life through whom we come to our Father. And this is the mystery! Through us, our Father and Christ come in the power of the Holy Spirit to others. "The true light" of which John has written shines through the lives of Jesus' people to challenge and overcome the darkness of this world. Those who have been found by Christ are used by him to find others.

I asked an undergraduate friend to write down why he believes. He wrote: "The reason why I have faith is really very simple. One summer after the Princeton strike had convinced me that man, even in his most noble dreams, is too often guided by hate and bent on destruction, I met some Christians. Now, these kids were just like myself in most ways. One had a problem with a boy friend on drugs, another was simply a very lonely person with a tremendous need for love. They were human beings hurt by the world. Nevertheless, they had a real, unmistakable power in their lives which gave them triumph over their problems and a sincere joy. They were alive and victorious, and I knew they had something I didn't. They said it was Jesus living in them that gave them this power. I knew they were telling the truth. I believed.

"So that's why I believe in Jesus Christ—I saw him alive in other people. Now, today, Jesus Christ keeps calling me to repeat what I said two years ago: I believe in Jesus Christ as my Lord. To say, 'I believe' is to let Christ live in me. For me, faith is the demand of the living Christ."

To this there are many, many people who can reply with a joyful "Amen."

CHAPTER FIFTEEN

Significant Books

This list of books is not intended to be complete. Those we suggest, however, are books that are the best of their kind, culled from thousands. Each will bring you a new insight and will guide you on your way.

The books are classified in six categories: Prayer and Meditation; Mysticism; Experience and Spiritual Guidance; Healing; Theology, History, Biography; and Novels.

To give you an indication of the kind of book it is and the area it covers, there is a brief description. We also rate the book as to difficulty: light, medium, heavy. A light book is not necessarily one that has less to give, for sometimes an author has that rare ability to express himself so that a difficult subject is more easily understood. The new Christian might be cautious, however, about wading into heavy books too soon, for he might become discouraged. It is better to wait. You will sense when you are ready.

If you have trouble locating books, ask bookstores and libraries for help.

Prayer and Meditation

Hayford, Jack W., *Prayer Is Invading the Impossible*. Logos. How to claim Calvary's total victory through prayer. Medium.

Herman, E., *Creative Prayer*. Harper & Row. A basic book. Light to medium.

Kildahl, John P., *The Psychology of Speaking in Tongues*. Harper & Row. A thorough coverage of this controversial subject. Light to medium.

Merton, Thomas, *Seeds of Contemplation*. Image. Excellent for guidance and meditation. Medium. Merton's last book, *Contemplation*, is not for beginners. Spare, brilliant. Heavy.

Quoist, Michel, *Prayers*. Sheed & Ward. Startling, realistic, beautiful meditations rooted in our times. Light to medium.

Smith, Bradford, *Meditation*.Lippincott. Broad coverage of this inward art. Medium.

Smith, Malcolm, *How I Learned to Meditate*. Logos. Author's description of how he learned principles of biblical meditation. Light.

Steere, Douglas V., *Dimensions of Prayer*. Harper & Row. Workbook on prayer. Medium.

Thomas a Kempis, *The Imitation of Christ*. Image. Outstanding classic of meditations. Medium.

Tompkins, Iverna, *God and I*. Logos. How to build a personal relationship with God through prayer. Light.

Mysticism

Underhill, Evelyn, *Mysticism*. Meridian. The definitive book on mysticism. Medium to heavy. *Practical Mysticism*, also by Underhill, is a smaller, easier book to read. Medium.

The Cloud of Unknowing. Penguin. Well-known anonymous classic of the mystical way. Medium to heavy.

Theologica Mystica. Pantheon. Another anonymous classic in the mystical approach to God. Heavy.

Experience and Spiritual Guidance

Bennett, Dennis and Rita, *The Holy Spirit and You*. Logos. A study-guide to the Spirit-filled life. Medium.

Buber, Martin, *I and Thou*. Translation by Walter Kaufmann. Scribner's. Best translation of this modern mystic's famous book. Medium to heavy.

Gordon, Ernest, *Meet Me at the Door*. Harper & Row. Answers for puzzled youth in unsettling times. Light.

St. John of the Cross, *Ascent of Mount Carmel. Spiritual Canticles*. Image. Both for the serious seeker. Heavy.

Kelley, Thomas, *A Testament of Devotion*. Harper & Row. Fine book for the beginner and others. A kind of continuous meditation that pulls us into God's love. Light.

Mumford, Bob, *Take Another Look at Guidance*. Logos. A study of divine guidance from the Scriptures and the author's personal experience. Medium.

Powers, Thomas E., *First Questions on the Life of the Spirit*. Harper & Row. Covers much information not found elsewhere. Medium.

St. Theresa of Avila, *Interior Castle*. Image. This rare saint had a gift for guiding souls. Medium to heavy.

Thornton, Martin, *Christian Proficiency*. Morehouse-Gorham. A practical and helpful book on setting up a "way of life." Medium.

Tournier, Paul, *A Place for You. The Meaning of Persons*. Harper & Row. This wise Christian psychiatrist has written some of the most lucid books concerning the problems of living. Only two are listed here. Any one of his other books will also be helpful and fascinating. Light to medium.

Healing

Casdorph, H. Richard, *The Miracles*. Logos. A physician documents miraculous healings—some related to the ministry of Kathryn Kuhlman. Medium.

Dearing, Trevor, *Supernatural Superpowers*. Logos. The Spirit of God moving today to save, heal, and deliver all those who turn to Jesus as their Lord. Light.

Kuhlman, Kathryn, *I Believe in Miracles*. Revell. The case histories of twenty-one men, women, and children healed of apparently incurable disease by the power of faith. Light.

Neal, Emily Gardiner, *A Reporter Finds God Through Spiritual Healing. God Can Heal You Now. The Lord Is Our Healer*. Morehouse-Barlow. For an understanding of God's healing powers, all these books are recommended. Light.

Theology, History, Biography

St. Augustine, *Confessions*. Image. Candid reflections by one of the world's great thinkers. Medium to heavy. Sherwood Wirt's *Love*

Song is a readable condensed translation of the *Confessions*. Harper & Row.

Baillie, John, *Invitation to Pilgrimage*. Oxford University Press. A deeply Christian theologian shares with us the foundations of his own faith. Medium.

Barclay, William, *Jesus As They Saw Him*. Harper & Row. Easily read impressions of Jesus by those who were there. Light.

————, *The Daily Bible Study*. Westminster. An excellent book series, each devoted to a New Testament book. Light to medium.

Barth, Karl, *God Here and Now*. London: Routledge. Easy introduction to the thought of a leading Christian thinker. See also *Evangelical Theology*. Doubleday. Light.

Bennett, Dennis, *Nine O'Clock in the Morning*. Logos. The autobiography of an Episcopal priest who received the baptism in the Holy Spirit, an experience that revolutionized his life and ministry. Light.

Brunner, Emil, *Our Faith*. Scribner's. A clearly argued exposition of our faith. See also *The Scandal of Christianity*. John Knox. Light.

Buckingham, Jamie, *Daughter of Destiny*. Logos. The candid biography of the famous evangelist Kathryn Kuhlman. Light.

Burghardt, S. J., and Lynch, W. F., *The Idea of Catholicism*. Meridian. Writings of major church thinkers. Medium.

Chesterton, G. K., *St. Francis of Assisi*. Image. Truly captures the world's most beloved saint. He is no saint of birds and birdbaths. Light.

Joad, C. E., *Recovery of Belief*. London: Faber. A philosopher's well-reasoned argument for his conversion to the Christian faith. Medium.

Joffroy, Pierre, *A Spy for God*. Harcourt Brace Jovanovich. A sympathetic portrait of a Christian who dared to witness as God's spy in Nazi Germany. Light.

Kierkegaard, Søren, *Fear and Trembling*. A good beginning for those willing to consider Kierkegaard's important teachings. Medium.

Lewis, C. S., *Screwtape Letters*. Macmillan. Amusing, sharp, critical look at the "average" Christian. All Lewis's books, including fiction, are recommended. A partial list includes *Mere Christianity*, *The Problem of Pain*, and *Surprised by Joy*. Light to medium.

Marbach, Ethel, *Family Liturgical Customs*. Abbey Press. Delightful series of five booklets packed with information on celebrating particular festivals and seasons. Filled with ideas and recipes. Light.

Muggeridge, Malcolm, *Jesus Rediscovered*. Doubleday. The experience of a famous skeptic turned believer. Light.

Read, David H. C., *Christian Ethics*. Lippincott. See also *Christian Faith*. Scribner's. Light.

Schweitzer, Albert, *Out of My Life and Thought*. Mentor. Autobiography of this modern genius and saint. Light.

Schweizer, E., *Jesus*. John Knox. Well-written account of Jesus' life and ministry. Medium.

Synan, Vinson, *Aspects of Pentecostal-Charismatic Origins*. Logos. Eleven leading scholars examine the roots and early growth of the greatest religious movement of the twentieth century. Heavy.

Temple, William, *About Christ*. London: S. C. M. Press. Archbishop William Temple of Canterbury was an outstanding thinker and teacher. The book introduces us to some of the great issues a Christian faces as he encounters the world of contemporary thought. See also his *Christian Faith and Life*. Allenson. Light.

Tydings, Judith, *Gathering a People*. Logos. Describes and illustrates the complete harmony between Catholic tradition and the current Charismatic renewal among Catholics. Heavy.

Novels

Many novels, though not explicitly religious, deal with religious themes and human values. We especially recommend the following: William Golding, *Lord of the Flies*; Ernest Gordon, *Somewhere To Go*; Graham Greene, *The Power and the Glory*; Nikos Kazantzakis, *The Greek Passion*; Alan Paton, *Cry, the Beloved Country*; John Steinbeck, *The Winter of Our Discontent*; J. R. R. Tolkien, *The Lord of the Rings*; Laurens Van Der Post, *The Seed and the Sower* and *Venture to the Interior*.

Index

For free information on how to receive
the international magazine

LOGOS JOURNAL

also Book Catalog

Write: Information - LOGOS JOURNAL CATALOG
Box 191
Plainfield, NJ 07061